The History of Chinese Philosophy Book 1

By Laszlo Montgomery

ISBN-13: 978-988-8769-94-0

© 2023 Laszlo Montgomery

HISTORY / Asia / China

EB182

All rights reserved. No part of this book may be reproduced in material form, by any means, whether graphic, electronic, mechanical or other, including photocopying or information storage, in whole or in part. May not be used to prepare other publications without written permission from the publisher except in the case of brief quotations embodied in critical articles or reviews. For information contact info@earnshawbooks.com

Published in Hong Kong by Earnshaw Books Ltd.

THE HISTORY OF CHINESE PHILOSOPHY

BOOK 1

LASZLO MONTGOMERY

CONTENTS

Introduction	VII
The History of Chinese Philosophy Part 1	1

Chinese Philosophy's Ancient Beginnings, Early Western Understanding of Chinese Philosophy, Intro to the ancient Chinese sages as role models, Karl Jaspers Theory of the Axial Age

The History of Chinese Philosophy Part 2	11

Pre-Confucian Philosophy during the Eastern Zhou, Yuzi, Guan Zhong, the concept of the Junzi and the rise of the Knights Errant, the Earliest Beginnings of the Ru School, Duke Huan of Qi as a benefactor to scholars

The History of Chinese Philosophy Part 3	21

The early life of Confucius, his service to the Lu State, Confucius meets Laozi, The Great Sage's reflections on the ideal ruler.

The History of Chinese Philosophy Part 4	33

Introduction to Confucius's disciples, Confucian core beliefs, the Confucian concept of the Junzi, a selection of quotes from the Analects

The History of Chinese Philosophy Part 5	47

Introduction to the School of Names, the Sophists, Deng Xi, Confucian classics become a pathway to a career in the government

The History of Chinese Philosophy Part 6	55

More Ru School philosophers: Mozi, Yang Zhu, Mengzi

The History of Chinese Philosophy Part 7	69

More about Mengzi and introducing Xunzi

The History of Chinese Philosophy Part 8	83

Legalism during the Qin, Shang Yang, Shen Buhai, Han Fei, Li Si

The History of Chinese Philosophy Part 9   97

Dong Zhongshu and the triumph of Confucianism during the Han Dyansty, Sima Tan and the Six Schools, The first explainers of Confucianism: Liu Xin, Wang Chong, Yang Xiong

The History of Chinese Philosophy Part 10   111

The end of the Han Dynasty, the rise of Buddhism and the rivalries between the three religions, The seeds of Neo-Confucianism are planted, Han Yu, Li Ao, Liu Zongyuan and the Daotong Lineage

History of Chinese Philosophy Complete Terms List   125

INTRODUCTION

The China History Podcast was launched in June of 2010. The original intention of the show was to offer American people a basic understanding of Chinese history. Recognizing a widespread lack of even the simplest awareness of Chinese history in the USA, Laszlo Montgomery used the relatively new medium of podcasting to make it convenient and easy for listeners to access the show snd satisfy their curiosity to learn about China.

Now more than twelve years later, The China History Podcast is listened to in more than a hundred countries with less than half of the listeners residing in the US. There are over two hundred hours of free content that introduces Chinese history from mythical to modern times. Besides popular Chinese imperial history and post Qing Dynasty history, the China History Podcast has presented hours of content focusing on the lives of Overseas Chinese and their rich history.

The show is listened to all over the world by English-speakers hungry for an entertaining and informative explanation of China's history delivered in an enjoyable non-academic style. So many listeners around the world are Chinese, many of them happy for an entertaining way to reconnect with their heritage.

For more than a decade there have been so many calls from listeners to provide the transcripts to the programs. They will do much to help listeners learn more about China. Laszlo is happy to work with Earnshaw Books to bring you the transcripts from selected shows of The China History Podcast. These will become a unique and enjoyable way to advance English understanding, perhaps re-learn some forgotten history and gain a foreigner's perspective of China's great history presented by someone who has appreciated Chinese culture since he was a small boy growing up in Chicago.

Laszlo Montgomery

The History of Chinese Philosophy Part 1

THE TRANSCRIPTS

SUMMARY

Chinese Philosophy's Ancient Beginnings, Early Western Understanding of Chinese Philosophy, Intro to the ancient Chinese sages as role models, Karl Jaspers Theory of the Axial Age

TRANSCRIPT

00:00 Hey Everyone, Laszlo Montgomery here. Welcome to the start of another CHP series that will trace the development of Chinese philosophy through the lives of about three dozen philosophers. Some we'll look at in greater depth than others. And we'll trace the historical timeline and see where philosophy in China began... how it developed and throughout this series we'll also examine the historic events going on in the background that were driving a lot of this thought.

00:31 Let me encourage you to download the infographic that accompanies this series and to keep it handy. And just in case you're not a fluent Mandarin speaker, please refer to the master list of terms at the teacup.media website. Just click on the convenient link at the show notes and that will get you access to the list of terms. You can download them, print them.

I

 THE HISTORY OF CHINESE PHILOSOPHY
PART 1

00:52 It's my hope that, as Will Durant said in his introduction to classical Chinese philosophy, that this "brief and superficial introduction leads you to study the Chinese philosophers themselves, as Goethe studied them, and Voltaire, and Tolstoy."

01:12 We look at these ancients and perhaps think... their world was so simple back then. They were so ignorant of so much knowledge and intellectual discovery that we take for granted in our day. Their circumstances compared to ours in the 21st century...what could we possibly have in common with these people from so long ago? Well, in examining the things they cared about and thought about it turns out we have quite a bit in common with them.

01:55 The backdrop for all the first part of this story was the Zhou Dynasty. We always hear about how old China is and this is pretty much the farthest back you can go in recorded Chinese history. Other than all the bronze ware, ironware and other relics made from inorganic materials, not much from that time survived down to our day. The Chinese invented paper but Cài Lún wouldn't launch the paper industry till the first century of the common era during the Hàn.

02:27 And all these eponymous works from these Zhou era thinkers, the Laǒzǐ, the Mèngzǐ, Xúnzǐ, Zhuāngzǐ, Lièzǐ, Mòzǐ, Hán Fēizǐ, how much of that material can accurately be attributed to each philosopher, if any of it? The earliest works that have survived so far were all dug out of Han dynasty tombs, long after these philosophers were dead.

THE HISTORY OF CHINESE PHILOSOPHY
PART 1

02:56 | All these texts that scholars said contained the words of Confucius and other Masters ran the gauntlet of twenty-five centuries of argument and reinterpretation. Did we in the 21st century even receive 1% of what these classical philosophers actually said? And for those who can't read Classical Chinese, and have to read these ancient texts in a foreign language, I wonder how much of the beauty, subtleties and perhaps true meaning behind a lot of the texts got papered over in translation?

03:32 | Féng Yǒulán, author of the ground-breaking A Short History of Chinese Philosophy, mentioned something interesting. He said "religion was to other civilizations what philosophy was to China," describing religion as simply philosophy that also contained superstitions, dogmas, rituals and institutions.

03:57 | Humanism, *rénběnzhuyì*, is what Confucius and other Chinese philosophers mainly concerned themselves with. Matters of a metaphysical nature... not as much, not at the beginning anyway. What mattered most in Chinese philosophy was worldly affairs and the role of humans in the big picture. Though there was plenty that was spiritual and mystical about Chinese philosophy, especially where Dàoism was concerned, practical matters such as ethics, morals, innate human knowledge and politics figured most highly amongst all the great thinkers.

04:38 | When the Analects of Confucius and other Zhou Era classical works made their way to Europe, they were most warmly received. What an eye opener that was for the intellectuals of the day! That these works even found

THE HISTORY OF CHINESE PHILOSOPHY
PART 1

their way to Europe was thanks to the Jesuit fathers in China, most prominently Ruggieri, Ricci, Schall von Bell and Verbiest. When they began to crack that nut and learn the language and study the ancient texts, for the first time Western readers got to hear these names like Kǒngfūzǐ and Mèngzǐ. And these Jesuits Latinized the names into Confucius and Mencius to allow Europeans to better know them.

05:23 So, thanks to these Jesuits and all their heavy lifting learning the language and translating the ancient texts that were available to them, all the great minds of the Enlightenment got to be the first generation of people in the West to read how these Chinese philosophers preached loving thy neighbor as thyself and doing unto others as you would like them to do unto you, centuries before these words could be read in Matthew 7:12.

05:52 Diderot had written of the Chinese, "These peoples are superior to all other Asiatics in antiquity, art, intellect, wisdom, policy, and in their taste for philosophy."

06:06 Voltaire wrote, "The body of this empire has existed four thousand years, without having undergone any sensible alteration in its laws, customs, language, or even in its fashions of apparel. The organization of this empire is in truth the best that the world has ever seen."

06:28 Yeah, these Enlightenment greats really put China on a pedestal... of course they all lived during the glory years of the Qing. No one was saying that in the late 19th century.

THE HISTORY OF CHINESE PHILOSOPHY
PART 1

06:40 | I'll bring to your attention all the most important works and just mention a little bit about them... Some, like the Lúnyǔ or Analects of Confucius, the Mèngzǐ, the Zhuāngzǐ, the Dàodéjīng of course. Those are the most famous and are quoted most often along with Sūnzǐ's Art of War, which we won't cover in this course. But there were many others as well.

07:02 | These texts are all filled with poems, dialogs, chronologies, pronouncements, aphorisms, parables, diagrams you name it. Some like the Zhuāngzǐ, the so-called Second Book of the Dao, stand on their own merits as works of literature, even in translation.

07:23 | The common golden thread that seems to run through every philosopher from Yùzǐ to Wáng Yángmíng seems to always boil down to the question of how should someone live their life so that it's a worthwhile one? Are humans predisposed toward good or evil? And how should we, the sovereign down to the village nobody, treat each other? How should we organize ourselves and live together with the hopes that our conduct and way of thinking will cause there to be no need for punishments or war?

07:58 | Poured into the foundation of classical Chinese philosophy were the stories and deeds of the greatest of China's ancient sage kings. And from earliest times the figures who were lionized more than any other, and who Confucius himself held up as the living ideals for what it meant to be a sage ruler, were three mythical emperors, Yáo, Shùn and Yǔ.

THE HISTORY OF CHINESE PHILOSOPHY
PART 1

08:27 And three figures who we know lived, Kings Wén and his two sons, King Wǔ and Zhōu Gōng, the Duke of Zhou. In all the thousands of years, there were many great emperors and leaders, but those six, they didn't live to see it, but all of them singly or collectively became a metaphor in Chinese culture and history for what it meant to contain all the virtues, in spades, and to be considered a sage-ruler.

08:58 As far as Yáo, Shùn and Yǔ were concerned, despite their mythical status in our day, the Zhou dynasty historians said they were in fact real and wrote with great certainty about who they were and when they lived. But the great historian Sīmǎ Qiān was as far away from the time of Yáo as he was from our day.

09:22 Confucius had said of Yáo, "concerning the good Yáo, it is said that he ruled China for one hundred years, the years of his life being one hundred ten and six. He was kind and benevolent as Heaven, wise and discerning as the gods. From afar his radiance was like a shining cloud, and approaching near him he was as brilliant as the sun. Rich was he without ostentation, and regal without luxuriousness. he wore a yellow cap and a dark tunic and rode in a red chariot, drawn by white horses. The eaves of his thatch were not trimmed, and the rafters were un-planed, while the beams of his house had no ornamental ends. His principal food was soup, indifferently compounded, nor was he choice in selecting his grain. He drank his broth of lentils from a dish that was made of clay, using a wooden spoon. His person was not adorned with jewels, and his clothes

THE HISTORY OF CHINESE PHILOSOPHY
PART 1

were without embroidery, simple and without variety. He gave no attention to uncommon things and strange happenings, nor did he value those things that were rare and peculiar. He did not listen to songs of dalliance, his chariot of state was not emblazoned... In summer he wore his simple garb of cotton, and in winter he covered himself with skins of the deer. Yet he was the richest, the wisest, the longest-lived and most beloved of all that ever ruled China."

10:59 We can see from the earliest times, when recorded history was just in its infancy, already the lines were being drawn about what qualities were good and what was decent, what was not. Confucius held Yáo up as a model. Why? He was plain, practical, had his two feet planted on the ground, wasn't swayed by luxuries and comforts, was devoid of selfish desires. So you can see early on, already what is "good" is being defined. This standard for what constitutes human decency was starting to be more clearly defined. Even back then, it was considered good taste and good form to live and act humbly, modestly, not ostentatiously.

11:53 So then, what was bad? If Yáo, Shùn and Yǔ were held up by many philosophers as paragons of virtue, who were the examples to avoid?

12:03 Confucius and later generations would point at two kings. And these two were among the earliest villains in Chinese history. They were Kings Jié of Xià and Zhòu of Shāng. These two in particular were held up as essentially the opposite of what could be said of Yáo.

# THE HISTORY OF CHINESE PHILOSOPHY
PART 1

12:16 | These two were the poster-boys of wicked kings in Chinese history. Jié's time on this earth is traditionally pegged at 1728-1625 BCE, the time of Hammurabi in Babylon and the Jewish exodus from Egypt and the later Hyksos invasion of that land. The other one, Zhòu or Zhòu Xīn, he was the last ruler of the Shang Dynasty.

12:41 | Both of these kings were remembered for their decadence that was only surpassed by their depravity, cruelty and inattention to the demands of their job and the needs of their people. They were both in the same league as Caligula or Commodus.

12:58 | Yeah, these two, Kings Jié and Zhòu, they were the gifts that kept on giving over the centuries, not only for Confucius to point to but other philosophers and politicians as well. Jié and Zhòu... they too got to become metaphors, but not in their own lifetimes.

13:17 | So the spectrum of excellence to ignominy ran from Yáo to Zhòu and then there was everything else in between.

13:26 | Later, the great thinkers of the Han Dynasty will come up with the notion of Tiānmìng or the Mandate of Heaven... When the ruler was more of a Yáo than a Zhòu, Heaven determined them fit to rule and this mandate was manifested in all kinds of positive ways. Usually with peace and prosperity throughout the land, as well as a dearth of natural disasters. And if the ruler turned out to be more of a Jié or a Zhòu, Heaven cut them loose by demonstrating its displeasure through any number of pandemics, disasters or astronomical phenomena.

THE HISTORY OF CHINESE PHILOSOPHY
PART 1

14:04　All these stories, who knows what's true or not? This is what tradition tells us. The Xia, the Shang... this was all prelude to the Zhou. The Zhou Dynasty, that's where the Big Bang happens for Chinese philosophy. And for three centuries or so, in this longest of all China's dynasties, comes the first part of our story.

14:27　In 1949 — a big year in Chinese history that was — German philosopher Karl Jaspers 1883-1969, came up with this theory about an Achsenzeit or Axial Age that took place in civilizations stretching from the Mediterranean to the East China Sea from about the 8th to the 3rd centuries BCE. Jaspers had pointed out that living in different places completely unawares of one another, all at the same time period were not just Confucius, Laozi, Mòzǐ, Zhuāngzǐ and Lièzǐ but also Pythagoras, Socrates, Plato, Aristotle, Homer. And in India, Hinduism and Jainism were thriving. Gautama Buddha was also walking around India. Zoroaster was teaching in Persia. In fact, the year of Zoroaster's death was the year Confucius was born. In the Holy Land, these were the times of the prophets Elijah, Isaiah, Jeremiah. It was a very tight bandwidth, when all these philosophers and thinkers lived.

15:44　That was the marquee fact of Jaspers theory of the Axial Age. These philosophers and founders of religions, arguably the first great thinkers produced by their respective ancient civilizations, all had their moment on this earth pretty much at about the same time. The lives of Confucius and the Buddha, only twelve years apart in age. Karl Jaspers said it this way: "The spiritual foundations of humanity were laid simultaneously

THE HISTORY OF CHINESE PHILOSOPHY
PART 1

and independently in China, India, Persia, Judea, and Greece. And these are the foundations upon which humanity still subsists today."

16:31 | Whether or not Jaspers' theory is true, we can't know for sure. It does have its critics. But surviving texts clearly show the most relevant issues that face human beings wherever they congregate in large numbers were being pondered and argued by all of these thinkers in all these places, at about the same time, for the first time.

16:57 | Okay, before we go any further, let's draw the curtains and call it a night. Next time we convene we'll look at pre-Confucian philosophy in China. Confucius passed in 479 BC. This was during the Eastern Zhou Spring and Autumn Period. Many historians draw a line in the Eastern Zhou that uses the death of the Great Sage as the demarcation point between the end of the Spring and Autumn and the start of the Warring States Period.

17:26 | The Warring States Period of the Eastern Zhou Dynasty lasted until 221 BC, the year King Yíng Zhèng of the Qín Kingdom founded the Qín Dynasty, China's first imperial dynasty where an emperor, not a king, ruled over a unified land. That's all for next time. Much more to come, seventeen more episodes in fact.

17:51 | This is Laszlo Montgomery signing off from fantastic LA in the state of California, welcoming you to come back again next time for another exciting episode of the China History Podcast.

 **The History of Chinese Philosophy Part 2**

THE TRANSCRIPTS

SUMMARY

Pre-Confucian Philosophy during the Eastern Zhou, Yuzi, Guan Zhong, the concept of the Junzi and the rise of the Knights Errant, the Earliest Beginnings of the Ru School, Duke Huan of Qi as a benefactor to scholars

TRANSCRIPT

00:00   Welcome back everyone. Laszlo Montgomery here, continuing on here with this lovely China History Podcast introduction to the history of Chinese Philosophy. As advertised last time, we're going to be looking at Pre-Confucian Philosophy during the Zhou Dynasty, the last of the three Bronze Age Dynasties of ancient China.

00:21   So when did China's philosophers make their first appearance? In the Chinese philosophy history timeline nothing of great significance happened until the Zhou Dynasty started breaking up in the late 8th century BCE. The date for the demise of the Western Zhou is usually pegged at 770-771 BCE when the ruling family was chased out of their capital near present day Xīān. They fled to Hénán province where Luòyáng is today. And thence began the Eastern or Latter Zhou Dynasty.

 THE HISTORY OF CHINESE PHILOSOPHY
PART 2

00:57 | And as far as Chinese classical philosophy goes, that's where everything really starts. No dynasty lasted longer than the Zhou, 1046 to 256 BCE. Seven hundred ninety years. The Western Zhou ran from 1046 to, as I said, 770-71 BCE and it continued on in a somewhat degraded state during the Eastern Zhou until 256 BCE. The first half of the Eastern Zhou was called the Spring and Autumn Period and the Second half, well, that was a violent and blood-dripping time in Chinese history and it's known as the Warring States Period.

01:42 | During the final phase of the Warring States period, there were seven states left standing from what were once dozens and dozens during the Western Zhou. And by 221 BCE there was only one, the Qín State, who had bested all others. And they were led at that time by King Yíng Zhèng, much better known as the first emperor of China, Qín Shǐhuáng.

02:08 | We'll look at the Qin later on. For now, let's sit back and make ourselves comfortable as we look at the Zhou Dynasty, Former and Latter, and see how all the ingredients in China were just right for this explosion of philosophic thought.

02:27 | Trying to scrape together enough grains of pre-Confucian philosophy isn't an easy thing to do. Yeah, there's fragments of writings and inscriptions that have been uncovered. But most of the time we don't know for sure who said what, and even when we have something, we're not sure what its intended meaning is.

THE HISTORY OF CHINESE PHILOSOPHY
PART 2

02:47 | The farthest back I was able to go was to the very genesis of the Zhou Dynasty, to the days of the venerable King Wén and his two sons, the older, King Wǔ and younger, Zhōu Gōng, the Duke of Zhou. Like Yáo, Shùn and Yǔ, this trinity from the founding years of the Zhou are held up by the Confucian Rú School of philosophers as the epitome of benevolence and virtue in a ruler. They did no wrong.

03:18 | This is all around 11th century BCE. King Wen lived from 1152 to 1056. Around that time lived a man named Yù Xióng who posterity has referred to as Master Yù or Yùzǐ. We know of Yùzǐ because some fragments of his writing appeared later on in history in a number of ancient classics and compendia, namely *The Book of Hàn* and in the Qīng dynasty Qiánlóng Emperor's encyclopedia to end all encyclopedias, the Sìkù Quánshū, just to name a couple.

03:55 | And not just Yùzǐ, quite a few philosophers are only remembered in the fragments of their teachings that managed to be saved, commented on and then mercifully inserted into some collection that kept the work alive.

04:10 | Now, we're only hearing this on the authority of China's greatest historian from ancient times, Sīmǎ Qiān, but Yùzǐ, who came from Jīngzhōu in Húběi, served as the *huǒ shī* for the first five Zhou kings. The *huǒ shī* was a ceremonial post at the royal court that involved anything having to do with fire. Back then, rituals carried a lot of weight and much faith was placed in them. So his role was significant at the time.

THE HISTORY OF CHINESE PHILOSOPHY PART 2

04:42   He was also referred to as a teacher and advisor to the ruling Jī clan, the founders of the Zhou Dynasty. They were all surnamed Ji. Yùzǐ had previously been in the employ of the Shāng rulers but defected to the Jī's and served them till his last days. It was supposedly Yùzǐ who was the first to say, "He who renounces fame has no sorrow."

05:09   Yùzǐ is not a household name in Chinese history or even Chinese philosophy for that matter. His philosophy is hard to discern. No surprise there. He wrote about constant changes and the cycles of the universe and nature. His twenty-two chapter work called *The Yùzǐ*, is slotted in the proto-Daoist category. Not exactly Daoism, but not anything else either.

05:39   But he also touched on certain matters that would be discussed, argued and debated for centuries after he left his earthly form. These concerned what made a ruler fit to rule? How to reward and punish? What made good politics? Nothing profound but, as I mentioned, scholars in the Later Zhou and in the Han considered Yùzǐ's words of sufficient enough import to keep his memory and scant content alive in the collected works they compiled for posterity.

06:12   You know, it's a miracle we have as much history of Chinese philosophy as we do. More got lost than discovered and we can only imagine how many Confucius's didn't make it past the Zhou or the Han before their work, no matter how significant and profound in its day, was lost and their lives forgotten.

THE HISTORY OF CHINESE PHILOSOPHY
PART 2

06:33 | This next person I wanted to mention, he's not really called a philosopher as much as he was a statesman. I am reluctant to not mention this man, who was of such great importance in Chinese history, that Confucius, said of him if it hadn't have been for the gifts conferred to the Chinese people by Guǎn Zhòng, we'd all be a bunch of barbarians.

06:59 | This person he was referring to, Guǎn Zhòng, he lived from 720 to 645 BCE. Confucius was born ninety-four years after Guǎn Zhòng's death, so he was an immediate beneficiary of Guǎn Zhòng's many contributions to political order, laws, Chinese culture and to philosophy as well.

07:19 | Guǎn Zhòng is remembered for many things. Historically, he was the prime minister to Duke Huán of the State of Qí. Qí Huán Gōng, the first of the Hegemons. These Hegemons were sort of like a *primus inter pares* for all feudal lords who swore fealty to the Zhou King. He spoke for them all and had the muscle power to give orders and maintain some semblance of order between all these future warring states.

07:50 | As the Duke of Zhou is held up as the ultimate example of the perfect regent, so Guǎn Zhòng is equally esteemed as the perfect prime minister, or right hand to the ruler. With Guǎn Zhòng at his side Duke Huán's Qí state became the most powerful force in Zhou Dynasty China.

08:12 | Under Guǎn Zhòng's steady guidance China transitioned from the Bronze Age to the Iron Age. He put the Qí

THE HISTORY OF CHINESE PHILOSOPHY
PART 2

fiscal house in order and got the entire state firing on all cylinders militarily, culturally and administratively. He helped establish a legal code that would incorrectly put him in the same pot as the Legalist philosophers Hán Fēi and Lǐ Sī. But he would have been more of a Confucianist than a Legalist.

08:42   Under Guǎn Zhòng, the whole concept of the "Chinese gentleman" began to take shape. Not the British version of what constitutes a gent. This is the Chinese version of the gentleman, called a *jūnzǐ*. A man of noble character, of virtue, an ideal man whose character embodied the virtue of benevolence and whose acts were in accordance with the rights and with rightness.

09:10   Guǎn Zhòng's *jūnzǐ* didn't have to come from the moneyed or privileged class. No big deal to hear that in our day, but back in the early 7th century BCE that was a new and revolutionary idea.

09:25   Being and acting in accordance with all that being a *jūnzǐ* meant, became like a religion to the aristocracy and this emerging group. And as Jaspers' Axial Age gathered speed, it was Guǎn Zhòng who got the pitch ready in China for what was to follow with the likes of Lǎozǐ, Confucius and all of their disciples.

09:50   During Guǎn Zhòng's time, Qí State became the model for this new and sophisticated land of opportunity where people could come to and study under the patronage system of the ruling house. Qí had become the first of these Zhou-era states to attract scholars and

THE HISTORY OF CHINESE PHILOSOPHY
PART 2

10:32 to patronize them and you know, as they said later on in history, created the environment where a hundred flowers could bloom and a hundred schools of thought might contend. The atmosphere for stimulating this kind of philosophical and intellectual discussion developed much quicker in the wake of Guǎn Zhòng.

10:32 We'll see next time, the preeminent intellectual institution in ancient China will get built there in Qí State. This is in today's northern Shandong province.

10:44 The History of Chinese philosophy really has its beginnings right when the political center broke down and the Zhou Dynasty kings lost their power. Once that gravitational force was lost, it became a long hard slog lasting centuries where the more powerful devoured the less mighty. As I said, what were once many dozens of these states and statelets, eventually got whittled down to seven. And then these seven would beat the you-know-what out of each other for generations on end. It was a miserable time.

11:21 And swearing loyalty to many of these vanquished feudal lords, who didn't make it to the final seven, who no longer had anyone to lord it over, were these hereditary warriors, knights. They weren't your average army grunts. These were educated men. And these suddenly unemployed knights became known, in English anyway, as Knights Errant. Errant in the Old French meant wandering. So a wandering knight, like a Japanese Ronin.

THE HISTORY OF CHINESE PHILOSOPHY
PART 2

11:53　In Mandarin, they were known as the *xiá shì* or just the *shì* class. And these educated soldier knights-errant grew in numbers very quickly as more of them found themselves on their own due to the defeat of their lord.

12:08　These Chinese knights errant, they became the heroes glorified in all the Jīn Yōng *wǔxiá* novels. Historian Sīmǎ Qiān put these guys on a pedestal. They were noble, totally selfless, ready to dive in and help the oppressed or peasant in distress. And as I said, they were educated, had studied the classics of their time and were schooled in all the major ceremonies and rituals. There's been a million movies made about these heroes.

12:43　These *shì* or *xiáshì* along with other educated nobles were the class that evolved into the Rú school of philosophers. Rú… .R-U. Confucius belonged to this category. In English we say Confucianism… but nobody uses that word in China… This school of thought that included Confucianism and others formed the Rú School. When you look up Rú in the dictionary it just says that it means Confucianism but in more ancient times it meant a scholar or a learned person.

13:19　The *shì* or scholar officials made up the core base of the Rú class. You could consider them the lowest of those who made up the top layers of society. These former knights were the ones who worked that layer of middle and lower-level civil bureaucrats in the government, your average Zhou Dynasty civil servant.

THE HISTORY OF CHINESE PHILOSOPHY
PART 2

13:42 | So in the century following all that, Guǎn Zhòng had laid the groundwork for while in the employ of Duke Huán of Qí, sprang these Rú philosophers, of which Confucius was just one of many.

13:57 | They became teachers when education became a path to social mobility. People of talent now for the first time in China had this potential yellow brick road to greener pastures, even if their relative wasn't a noble. Education became the fast track to the good time.

14:18 | Yeah, once the Western Zhou ended, the good times began to appear farther and farther away in China's historical rear-view mirror. Life became very bumpy and unpredictable. And that's when people began to start discussing and arguing, what was the best way to get out of this mess?

14:39 | Back then, they believed in a top down approach and that it all began with the ruler. So amidst all the unpleasantness up and down the Yellow River Valley, people began to have all these discussions. They discussed very weighty matters like what makes the best ruler, how shall we organize ourselves so that harmony in society is achieved? What was the best system of government? All pretty boring and simple stuff in our day. But back then, when all these ideas were fresh, new and without precedent, it was a very big deal.

15:16 | Because of the ancient texts and oral histories passed on from earlier times, people knew there was a period in China when peace was enjoyed by everyone and the

# THE HISTORY OF CHINESE PHILOSOPHY
PART 2

kings were virtuous. The country prospered. Now, it was just the opposite, it was every feudal lord for himself. And some serious debate started happening about where the Han People and their civilization should go from here.

15:43 Into this state of affairs that defined the 6th century BCE in China stepped all the names we know and love, Laŏzĭ and Confucius most notably. And these two great thinkers, before they left this earth, gave posterity plenty to think about as far as how to deal with these tumultuous times in the Eastern Zhou.

16:07 And that is the setup for next time. We're going to look at a few of these dozens and dozens of schools of thought that became known, and the Băi Jiā or hundred schools. We'll examine the life and times of a few of these philosophers during the time of Confucius.

16:23 And until that time, *mes amis*, this is Laszlo Montgomery signing off from the city of night, in the state of California, entreating you to come back again next time for another exciting episode of the China History Podcast.

The History of Chinese Philosophy Part 3

THE TRANSCRIPTS

SUMMARY

The early life of Confucius, his service to the Lu State, Confucius meets Laozi, The Great Sage's reflections on the ideal ruler.

TRANSCRIPT

00:00 Hey everyone, Laszlo Montgomery here. My deepest thanks for tuning in to the China History Podcast. We're still talking about the History of Chinese Philosophy. We now enter the fabulous 5th and 6th centuries BC and the age of philosophy is flourishing for the first time in human history, and not just in China. Greece, Persia, India and on the eastern shores of the Mediterranean… all over.

00:27 Two years after Confucius left his earthly form, Pericles was born in Greece. Humankind, after advancing from our most primitive stages of development to where things were in the 700's, 600's and 500's BCE, for the first time, and again I want to emphasize and re-emphasize, simultaneously in all these centers of human civilization, they all began to argue and debate these most fundamental of philosophical questions.

 THE HISTORY OF CHINESE PHILOSOPHY
PART 3

00:58 | I mentioned the State of Qí in Shāndōng province being the first place in China where the rulers began to patronize scholars and find uses for them. Thanks to Guǎn Zhòng's stewardship of the Qí State a century prior, Qí was now considered the Ivy League so to speak, of higher learning in China. Thinkers and teachers from all parts of Zhou Dynasty China flocked to Qí where all the intellectual action was.

01:28 | Confucius was just one of the many scholars and teachers who made the pilgrimage to Qí. Qí State was located next door to where Confucius made his bed every night, in Lǔ, the southern portion of Shāndōng.

01:41 | In Chinese, Confucius is known as Kǒngzǐ. Most of you may have noticed all these "zǐ's" coming as a suffix at the end of a lot of names and eponymous philosophical works. In Chinese that's called a zūnchēng, like an honorific or respectful term added to your surname. This *zǐ* means master. Since Confucius's name was Kǒng Qiū, surname Kǒng, this *zūnchēng* of *zǐ* was added to his surname Kǒng, and we know him forever more as Kǒngzǐ. Master Kong. That's all there is there with that. So Mèngzǐ, Master Mèng. Xúnzǐ, Master Xún. Sūnzǐ, the guy who wrote *The Art of War*, Master Sūn.

02:33 | So let's talk about the legend of Kǒngzǐ. Probably none of this is historically accurate but what the hey. This was the Zhou dynasty. I'm sure not a single one of you will be surprised that for Confucius, as it is with almost but not quite everybody who came before Sīmǎ Qiān, all we have for primary sources is what The Record of the

THE HISTORY OF CHINESE PHILOSOPHY
PART 3

Grand Historian has revealed. And Sīmǎ Qiān had to pretty much go with whatever he could glean from what Master Kong's disciples said, as well as from Mèngzǐ and in another major work of the day called Zuǒ Zhuàn 左轉, *The Commentary of Zuǒ*.

03:11　That Confucius lived has never been disputed. He ain't no Lǎozǐ. But the details are all in line with what you'd expect from this historical age. It all makes for scintillating reading, but how much of it is factual, if any, no one can know for sure. He was born in the Year of the Dog, was a tall, strange-looking man, his father was many years older than his mother and passed away when young Kǒng Qiū was only three.

03:40　Not coming from money, it was an impoverished upbringing and like many of the mothers of the sages, Madame Kǒng, though not much is mentioned about her, was a model of sacrifice, and propriety.

03:55　Confucius traced his ancestry back to Shāngqiū in Sòng State, eastern Hénán and a tad of Western Shandong. As I said, he was named Kǒng Qiū. Three generations before the birth of Kǒngzǐ in 551 BCE, his family had migrated north to Lǔ State, southern Shandong, near the city of Qūfù.

04:18　That's why Qūfù is so important. Confucius's birthplace. That's the location of the main Confucian Temple. Duke Āi of Lǔ, a year after Confucius's passing, ordered the Kǒng Miào, the Temple of Confucius, to be built there. Still there today twenty-five hundred years later. A major

THE HISTORY OF CHINESE PHILOSOPHY PART 3

tourist attraction in China as well. There're Confucian temples everywhere in China and around the world. But the one in Qūfù is the main one, the St. Peter's so to speak.

04:53 Well, there's not a lot of rice in this gruel so we can skip ahead and say that Kǒngzǐ married at nineteen, divorced at twenty-three and remained a swinging single for the rest of his days. And when his upstanding and virtuous mother passed away, Confucius dutifully mourned her for three years, a number purposely chosen to allow one to reflect, during this period of mourning, on their own first three years of life when they depended on their parents for their very life and survival.

05:27 Time to give the years back as a sign of mourning and filial piety.

05:31 At age twenty-two, which would have been north or south of 520 BCE, Confucius began his teaching career and hung a shingle outside his residence. He had no trouble attracting students.

05:44 And just as Confucius was beginning his career, over in present-day Bihar State in India, the Buddha had only just recently attained enlightenment.

05:55 At the school run by Kǒngzǐ, which gained a great amount of repute in and around that part of Zhou Dynasty China, there were three subjects taught: history, poetry and rules of propriety.

THE HISTORY OF CHINESE PHILOSOPHY
PART 3

06:08 | Confucius said, "A man's character was formed by the *Book of Odes*, developed by the Rites and perfected by music." The *Book of Odes*, the *Book of Rites* and the *Book of Music* were all ancient texts that were studied during the Zhou. So successful was Confucius as a teacher, he became the first of his profession to amass as many students as he did... over three thousand.

06:36 | The standard curriculum that developed became known as the Six Arts. The *Liù Yì*. These were rituals, music, archery, chariot riding, calligraphy and math. That traditional Chinese respect for knowledge and education and for those who were educated began here. Confucius till his dying day promoted it. He thought the best things anyone could do was find a good teacher and imitate that teacher in their words and actions.

07:09 | One of his students introduced Master Kǒng to someone at the Zhou Dynasty court. And so began Kǒngzǐ's career in the Lǔ government, based conveniently in his home in Qūfù. But much to Confucius's chagrin, rather than the Duke of Lǔ being in charge, the capital at this time was controlled by a cabal of three corrupt and self-serving noble families. They were called the Three Huán Families. Confucius pined for a day when the Duke of Lǔ's power could be restored. That Lǔ was controlled for the benefit of three corrupt and morally bankrupt families went against everything Confucius called for in his ideology.

07:56 | Later on, Confucius will make the mistake of meddling in these heated rivalries between the Three Huán

THE HISTORY OF CHINESE PHILOSOPHY
PART 3

Families of Lǔ and he ended up on the wrong side of Viscount Jì Sūn, Jì Sūn Shì of one of these three powerful clans. Confucius had committed the error of meddling in politics and not keeping his mouth shut. And for this transgression, Confucius would, around 496 BCE, have to leave town and lay low for a while.

08:27 But initially, when he began his stint in the Lǔ government in 501 BCE, Confucius was lauded for his performance, winning accolades for his honesty and integrity. By 498 Duke Dìng of Lǔ, Lǔ Dìng Gōng, made Confucius Acting Superintendent of Public Works. Again, the record states that he did many laudable things during his brief tenure.

08:52 He moved on to the post of Minister of Crime. The most notable thing I read about his brief time in this post was that Confucius sentenced a man to die once. I thought this was far out, especially when you examine this through a 21st century lens.

09:09 Confucius said he pronounced the man guilty because, "he was capable of gathering about him large crowds of men; that his arguments could easily appeal to the mob and make perversity respectable; and that his sophistry was sufficiently recalcitrant to take a stand against the accepted judgments of right."

09:31 No matter which country we reside in, in our past history this kind of demagoguery is something many of us have a passing acquaintance with.

THE HISTORY OF CHINESE PHILOSOPHY
PART 3

09:41 | Again, the details of Kǒngzǐ's career in government are the stuff of legends that were written about him centuries after his passing. There are historians who dispute all of this.

09:53 | Once on an official visit to the capital Luòyáng... this was in 518 BCE, while Confucius was still in the employ of the Duke of Lǔ... he sought out an appointment with no less a personage than Lǎozǐ himself. Now, we'll discuss Lǎozǐ in detail in another episode. But this legendary meeting of the two greatest philosophers of ancient China was well documented in the Record of the Grand Historian.

10:18 | Lǎozǐ by 518 BCE had already established quite a name and reputation throughout the land and after meeting with the Old Master, Confucius was quite moved. When Confucius came face to face with the great Lǎozǐ and asked his advice on certain matters of ceremony and ritual, Lǎozǐ famously and cryptically replied:

10:39 | "What you are studying and teaching now is all from ancient men who died a long time ago and even their bones have rotted away. Those written words are in fact only their footprints, neither their shoes nor their feet, let alone what was in their minds. Don't regard their words as some sort of unbreakable dogma.

11:00 | Secondly, as a man of virtue and knowledge, you can have your own cart and live a luxurious life. If the time does not permit, it will be perfectly okay as long as you can manage to survive.

THE HISTORY OF CHINESE PHILOSOPHY
PART 3

11:12 Thirdly, once I was told of an old saying: a good merchant does not show his goods and a man of utmost virtue is always simple. It will do you good if you cut off your pride, get rid of your greed, reduce your haughtiness, throw away some of your ambitions. It will serve your family better, and it will serve your state better if you are not too stubborn no matter whenever, wherever, and whatever. That is all I have to say to you."

11:44 This puzzled Confucius at first, but this brief moment in time that he was fortunate to spend with Lǎozǐ transformed Confucius. As he reflected more and more on these words and their vague meaning, it's written in the Shǐ Jì that he had said, "Birds can fly but will fall at the hunter's arrow. Fish can swim but will be hooked by the fisherman. Beasts can run but will drop into people's nets and traps. There is only one thing that is out of man's reach. That's the legendary dragon. A dragon can fly into the sky, ride on clouds, dive into the ocean. A dragon is powerful yet so intangible to us. Lao Tzu is a dragon, and I'll never understand him."

12:36 Lǎozǐ was much older than Confucius, but their lives did have some overlap, and if you read the stories or grew up with them, their paths crossed a couple times. Confucius held Laozi in the highest esteem. Remember in the Old Master's lifetime, nobody was talking about Daoism or pointing at Lǎozǐ as the founder of some school of thought.

13:02 These vignettes of legendary meetings between Lǎozǐ and Kǒngzǐ make for great reading but how the Old

THE HISTORY OF CHINESE PHILOSOPHY
PART 3

Master impacted Master Kong's thought, I can't say for sure. But that was their most famous encounter.

13:16 After he returned to Lǔ, Confucius was forlorn to see how far his home state had fallen. The gory details of the demise of the State of Lǔ are chronicled in the Chūnqiū or Spring and Autumn Annals, again supposedly written by Confucius. He had simply concluded that this degradation of the State and then society at large was the kind of thing that happened in the absence of a ruler who lacked these necessary virtues.

13:49 Confucius said time and again, place a ruler on the throne who was virtuous, benevolent, wise and reverent. *Rén*, humaneness and *yì*, righteousness, would be this ruler's underlying qualities. And the ruler's skillful stewardship of the state and their ethical example would serve as the model for everyone to follow. And the ruler's goodness would inspire others to follow his example and never would they be required to rely on using force or meting out punishments...

14:24 To Confucius, it was essential that a ruler must be someone who emulated Yáo and Shùn in the simplicity of their royal court and the number of adornments they might display around the palace or wear on their person. Wealth would be equitably distributed amongst the populace. Confucius was anti-war and even anti-foreign-relations. He said, be self-sufficient for all your needs and then there will never be any need to engage in potential conflicts with those beyond China's borders.

THE HISTORY OF CHINESE PHILOSOPHY
PART 3

14:59 After things got too hot in Lǔ for Confucius, he and a bunch of his disciples packed up and left Qūfù, under pressure from the corrupt ruling nobles. Kǒngzǐ decided to wander the lands and seek out this leader who had those basic qualities and who would listen to what he had to say, find merit in his words and then, presumably, hire him as an official adviser of sorts to help the ruler implement his ideology. He wouldn't return to Lǔ until 484 BCE.

15:34 As I mentioned, there were no shortage of people like Kǒngzǐ walking the streets of China's capitals. He was just one of many learned men who went from state to state offering their consulting services. Mèngzǐ, Xúnzi and many of the great Warring States philosophers did the same exact thing. These teachers or wise masters all had their own ideas about how everything in society should be organized, administered and how the ruler should act in order to maintain peace and harmony in their lands... and lead his people by example.

16:14 And the thing for rulers to do back then was to invite these wandering philosophers to their respective states, to have these discussions about – from a macro perspective at least – how best to run their kingdom.

16:29 For more than a decade, Confucius was one of these wandering scholar/teachers. The actual number of years he was outside Lǔ and teaching in all these other places is disputed. He went from city to city searching for his Holy Grail, a virtuous ruler who he could coach and advise.

THE HISTORY OF CHINESE PHILOSOPHY
PART 3

16:50 | A few rulers he visited kicked his tires and tried him out, the Duke of Wèi and others in Cài, Chén and Sòng states. He also went to Chǔ. Either these dukes or princes weren't interested or Confucius found them not worth his time. Why? Because they were all lost causes who lacked all the most basic virtues and qualities that were required of a sage ruler.

17:17 | When Confucius's travels took him to Qí State, the ruler at that time would have been Qí Jǐng Gōng, Duke Jǐng. A particular snippet from his time with Duke Jǐng concerned this other well-known story about when the Duke asked the Great Sage what makes a good government. Master Kǒng famously answered him this way: "There is a good government when the prince is the prince, the minister is the minister, when the father is the father and the son is the son." I think this one actually makes the Confucian Quotes Top Ten. When everyone knows their place and acts accordingly, you can count on a good and stable government.

18:02 | And with that little pearl of wisdom, let's slip the proverbial bookmark back in until another time. We're still very early in the game, so I encourage you to not start folding up the lawn chairs just yet. Please consider coming back again in Part 4. You won't be sorry you did. This is Laszlo Montgomery, signing off from Los Angeles in America's Golden State. And I am welcoming you with open arms to come back again next time for another exciting episode of the China History Podcast.

The History of Chinese Philosophy Part 4

THE TRANSCRIPTS

SUMMARY

Introduction to Confucius's disciples, Confucian core beliefs, the Confucian concept of the Junzi, a selection of quotes from the Analects

TRANSCRIPT

00:00	Welcome back everyone, Laszlo Montgomery here, thanks for tuning in to the China History Podcast. Part 4 today in this eighteen part series that looks at the history of Chinese Philosophy. We're still in the Spring and Autumn Period. This was during China's Bronze Age. And we're talking about Confucius. So let's pick up from where we left off last time in Part 3.
00:24	Confucius is still living on the road, searching for that perfect ruler. The life of an itinerant philosopher, living on the run, was a hard one. People from rock stars to traveling salesmen will attest to that. Plenty of times, Kǒngzǐ and his entourage of disciples faced these life-and-death situations. And I'm sure the transport back in the early 500's BCE wasn't that great either.
00:51	As an advisor to Qí ruler Duke Jǐng, Kǒngzǐ wasn't being taken seriously and, like with everyone else, he

THE HISTORY OF CHINESE PHILOSOPHY
PART 4

found this ruler of Qí lacking in virtue. Duke Āi of Lǔ, who reigned 494-467 BCE, brought Confucius back home again in 483, or so says the *Zuǒ Zhuàn*. Believe it or not, there was this sort of rivalry between Lǔ and Qí. Rulers of both rival states vied with each other to keep the famous Confucius in their camp, even though they didn't heed his advice. Each would try and entice Kǒngzǐ to come to their capital to teach.

01:34   But Master Kong returned to Lǔ for good. And it was there, with Confucius pushing 70 years old, he finished off his days, teaching and being accorded all the reverence and respect that many a great teacher has enjoyed over the millennia. His last years were spent working on the *Book of Songs*, also called the *Book of Odes*, the *shī jīng*. He also devoted a great teal of time on the *Shàng Shū*, the Book of Documents as well as the *Chūn Qiū*, the Spring and Autumn Annals, from which we get the name of that half of the Eastern Zhou. The *Chūn Qiū* chronicles the years of Lǔ State from 722 to 481 BCE.

02:15   Confucius also spent his final years trying to figure out the *Yì Jīng*. That he began to study it so late in life was one of Master Kǒng's dying regrets. What he wrote about the *Yì Jīng* had some rather profound consequences.

02:29   Kǒngzǐ didn't know it back then, that he'd end up as famous and long lasting as he ended up being, longest social and political philosophy in history, you could argue. I suppose he might have felt thankful having achieved, in his own time, some degree of success as a teacher of students who had risen far in the government.

THE HISTORY OF CHINESE PHILOSOPHY
PART 4

02:49 | But as far as his greatest goal of finding that one virtuous ruler who he could latch onto and guide, Confucius never got to achieve that. In fact, in some places Kǒngzǐ went to, he was downright disparaged and physically mistreated.

03:06 | When he passed in 479 BCE, he was given quite a sendoff by his disciples, who were said to number something like seventy-seven. Some were more famous than others. His grandson Zǐsī was maybe the most famous. Confucius had a son, but I guess the only achievement this son had was siring Zǐsī. His disciples mourned him for three years. I'm sure Confucius would have insisted, even through this was a period of time only reserved for one's parents' passing.

03:37 | At the time of his death, Kǒngzǐ was just one of many teachers and philosophers in China. But like Elvis and James Dean, Confucius ended up much bigger in death than in life.

03:50 | What followed in the wake of Confucius's life was an explosion in Chinese philosophy and philosophers. By Kǒngzǐ's time, this became the preferred career for many an aspiring scholar. Luòyáng for a while became the Silicon Valley of philosophers. Mèngzǐ was one of the many who made the trip there.

04:12 | Soon after the Great Sage's passing, Chinese history entered the Warring States period, a time of great violence and misery but also an extremely fertile period for philosophy. The Hundred Schools of Thought argued

THE HISTORY OF CHINESE PHILOSOPHY
PART 4

	everything and many books were written. Well, paper wasn't invented yet, but strips of bamboo was what they used. A whole kaleidoscope of philosophical writings burst onto the scene.
04:40	Although Confucius enjoyed some degree of shine in his own lifetime, the true reason why he managed to attain the longevity he did was all due to his disciples. How far might Christianity have gone without Matthew, Mark, Luke and John, and the Apostles? Same with Confucianism.
04:59	Yeah, later on there are certain works that are attributed to Confucius but he personally didn't leave any books behind. It's said Confucius played some role in editing and compiling many of the canonical texts that became known as the Thirteen Confucian Classics, the *Shísān Jīng*. He's also credited with producing The Ten Wings or Commentaries to the Zhōu Yì, the Changes of Zhou.
05:24	But honestly, everything we have, that managed to make it to the modern age, were the teachings and quotations of Confucius as remembered and written down by disciples and others who followed the Great Sage a century or even centuries later.
05:42	Confucius did not dwell so much on a person's innate nature. Are you born good or born bad? Mèngzǐ said good. Xúnzǐ said not so. But Kǒngzǐ... he didn't make this such a big issue. He was a "big picture" person, I guess you could say.

THE HISTORY OF CHINESE PHILOSOPHY
PART 4

05:58 Without getting lost in all the quotes that I extracted from the Four Books and the *Lúnyǔ* in particular, let me try to encapsulate what Confucius was all about. What was of importance to him? How did he look at things?

06:11 If you love metaphysics, Kǒngzǐ isn't your philosopher. He was concerned only with human affairs. And his passion was taking his thought and applying it to the government leadership, operation and administration. His focus was on matters like, how everyone in society should conduct themselves, at home, in public and in certain other situations. Etiquette was everything.

06:38 Of the Thirteen Confucian Classics, three deal only with this subject. *The Rites of Zhou, Ceremonies and Rites* and the *Book of Rites*, the *Zhōulǐ, Yílǐ* and *Lǐjì*.

06:51 Confucius believed all these ancient rites that had been ignored or carried out half-heartedly for so many years, had to be done right. All of these rites, ancestor worship included, had to be done with all seriousness. You had to really show up and be in the moment. That's why things had turned to you-know-what. Rulers and top officials demonstrated the worst regard for morality and ethics and setting an example for their subjects. So it was no wonder the character of the *lǎobǎixìng*, the people, had also degraded.

07:29 If you would ask Confucius what kind of a teacher he was, he'd tell you he didn't teach anything. All he did was re-introduce the wisdom and examples, and the Dào of the ancient sage rulers, and Confucius pointed

THE HISTORY OF CHINESE PHILOSOPHY
PART 4

to them, Yáo most of all, as we saw last episode, and he said these people were worth emulating, especially in these dark times in the late Spring and Autumn period. And the reason for lack of peace throughout the land was because everyone, the rulers most of all, had strayed too far from the perfect example set by Yáo.

08:06 Kǒngzǐ looked at the family as the national social system of China. Everything, as I said, began with the ruler who sets the moral example to his subjects. Morality, *dé*, so central to Confucian thought. The ruler's *dé*, in the Confucian way of thinking, rubbed off on the people.

08:27 And the people, seeing the moral example of their ruler passed this decency, this idea of *dé*, on to the younger generations. We translate *dé* as morality but it goes beyond that. Its morality and more.

08:43 Confucius said, "One who rules by moral force may be compared to the North Star – it occupies its place and all stars pay homage to it."

08:53 It was totally up to the family and no one else to teach their children and get this generation involved in perpetuating these old traditions. These rituals of *Lǐ*, this was the mechanism that united the state, the people, and heaven, all inclusively. Everyone was in it together. This idea will be advanced in leaps and bounds over the centuries that followed. It was up to the family, most importantly perhaps, to pass on to the next generation, knowing how to carry out and participate in all these traditional ceremonies and rituals and knowing your

THE HISTORY OF CHINESE PHILOSOPHY PART 4

place and your role inside the family and outside the family.

09:36 I'm sure many of you are familiar with the Five Bonds, the *wǔ cháng*. This was one of the hallmarks of Confucianism. In order of importance these five relationships were between ruler to the ruled, father to son, husband to wife, elder brother to younger brother and friend to friend.

09:57 You can say this kind of thinking had some staying power, lasting into modern times, especially with the last four of the five. Mobility in those BCE days, social or otherwise, was limited. People stayed where they were.

10:11 These knights errant or *Wǔxiá* wanderers I mentioned in Part 1, they were a tiny fraction of the population. Generally speaking, back then, there was none of this leaving the village to go work in a coastal city. The Civil Service exams hadn't been invented yet. Nobody went anywhere, and it was within this context that Kǒngzǐ, and all of these early philosophers, produced their thought.

10:36 The dynamic of that time shaped their thought every much as the events of the last years of the Qīng Dynasty clear through to May 4th, 1919 shaped Máo Zédōng Thought. These philosophers were very much products of their times.

10:52 As a remedy to all of these 5th century BCE ills, Kǒngzǐ taught the Five Constants and the Four Virtues. These

THE HISTORY OF CHINESE PHILOSOPHY
PART 4

qualities were the essence of what constituted the *Zhēnrén* or the Perfect Person. Confucius said that of The Five Constants, the two that mattered most were *Rén* and *Yì*, benevolence and righteousness. Rounding out the list were *Lǐ*, etiquette, *Zhī*, knowledge and *Xìn*, integrity. The Four virtues were Loyalty, Filial piety, self-control and for the second time, righteousness. Do the right thing. Being righteous, that was both a Constant and a Virtue.

11:38   You know I couldn't help but recall from my youth, Highlights Magazine. They had this comic strip called Goofus and Gallant, two brothers, you can guess which one was the good one and which was the ne'er-do-well. It was written in a way that said Goofus does it this way and Gallant does it that way.

11:58   Confucius, in the Analects, had so many stories that illustrated the difference between what he called the *xiǎorén*, the Small Person or Lower Person, compared with that of the *jūnzǐ*, the gentleman or Higher Person. Stuff like, "What the higher man seeks in himself, the lower man seeks in others."

12:18   I mentioned in last episode, many centuries before Jesus or Hillel Ha Gadol, Kǒngzǐ had this exchange between himself and his disciple Zǐ Gòng who asked, "Is there one word with which to act in accordance throughout a lifetime?" The Master said, "Is not reciprocity such a word? What you do not want done to yourself, do not do to others."

THE HISTORY OF CHINESE PHILOSOPHY
PART 4

12:43   And furthermore, Confucius said when performing, what Rabbi Hillel might have called a mitzvah, Confucius said do the good deed for the sake of doing it as a natural reaction, out of the true goodness of your heart. If you do someone a solid for the sake of some hidden agenda or to acquire future favors or gains of some sort, that's what a *xiǎorén* does, a small person. That's worse than not doing the deed at all.

13:11   Surely you've seen on Twitter when someone talks up a good deed they did, feeding the homeless perhaps, and they frame it in a way that screams out, Hey! Look what I did! Then they get shredded online with all this invective that unbeknownst to them, is very Confucian. They call them out and say they're calling attention to themselves for doing a good deed. It negates the whole act. Do it to do it, not to make yourself look like some sort of hero. The *jūnzǐ*, the gentleman, was the opposite of the *xiǎorén* in every way. There's no female *jūnzǐ*. Confucius wasn't a feminist, let's just say that.

13:49   Time and again throughout the writings of Kǒngzǐ he spoke about the *jūnzǐ*. The two Chinese characters "*jūn*" and "*zǐ*" literally translate to Prince's son.

14:01   The *jūnzǐ*, or Chinese gentleman, had it all in one single package. Contained in his physical and spiritual person was someone who always knew how to act appropriately in every situation, someone who had all the virtues and traits one needed to properly follow the Dào. Not the Dàoist Dào, the Confucian Dào, the Confucian Way of how a human ought to live their lives and conduct

THE HISTORY OF CHINESE PHILOSOPHY
PART 4

themselves as taught to posterity by the sage kings of old.

14:33 The acts of a *jūnzǐ* are repeatedly discussed in the Confucian Analects. He held them up as the ethical nobility. As I said, they need not come from the upper classes. In this world that Confucius lived, what mattered was your deportment. Example after example is given about how a *jūnzǐ* acts and does things and how a *jūnzǐ* thinks. And it's always the *xiǎorén*, the Small Person, who is held up as the gentleman's shameful opposite.

15:06 A *jūnzǐ* understands what is moral. The small man understands what is profitable. Confucius says the *jūnzǐ*, as opposed to the Small Person, had the following traits: 1. In regard to the use of their eyes, they are anxious to see clearly, 2. In regard to their countenance, they are anxious that it should be benign, 3. In regard to their demeanor, they are anxious that it should be respectful, 4. In regard to their speech, they are anxious that it should be sincere, 5. In regard to doing business they are anxious that it should be done reverently careful, 6. In regard to what they doubt, they are anxious to question others, 7. When they are angry, they think of the difficulties their anger may involve them in, 8. When they see gain to be made, they thinks of righteousness. Can you imagine a world where everyone thought this way?

16:02 The way that Confucius called for an orderly society with a number of social classes where everyone knew their place and nobody rocked the boat, was probably a good

THE HISTORY OF CHINESE PHILOSOPHY
PART 4

idea at the time. Considering the violence and random chaos of the Warring States Period, it was natural to hope for solutions that offered first and foremost, something that curbed violence and promoted tranquility. Even in today's most violent and unstable regions of the world, some people are willing to lower the bar as far as their personal hopes and aspirations for the sake of peace and a cessation of violence.

16:38 Let me give you some quotes from the *Lúnyǔ*. This is known in the English-speaking World as *The Analects of Confucius*. Basically it's a collection of sayings that are attributed to Kǒngzǐ. It's believed that they were conversations Kǒngzǐ had with his disciples and that not long after the passing of the Great Sage they were written down. So we can believe if we choose to, that if these aren't the actual words of Kǒngzǐ, they at least contain the spirit of what he taught. Not all but most of the Chinese classics that we can find today were written in the Hàn Dynasty. The original texts have all either been lost or destroyed and the final form that most of these classics took in the Hàn Dynasty don't match up exactly to the Zhou Dynasty versions. Confucius would make these statements and then endless discussion would follow about what he said and meant... This resulted in all kinds of exciting philosophical ideas that would come out of these core statements.

17:40 Here's some of Kǒngzǐ's greatest hits. Some of you might hear these words and be reminded of some of the lessons you learned in Sunday School...

THE HISTORY OF CHINESE PHILOSOPHY
PART 4

17:48 | "Respect yourself and others will respect you."

17:52 | "To be wealthy and honored in an unjust society is a disgrace."

17:57 | "Fine words and an ingratiating demeanor are seldom associated with true virtue."

18:03 | "When the wind blows, the grass bends." Here Kǒngzǐ means if the ruler is virtuous and benevolent he is like the wind and his force will naturally impact the people who are in this instance, the grass.

18:17 | "Lead the people with administrative injunctions and put them in their place with penal law, and they will avoid punishments but will be without a sense of shame. Lead them with excellence and put them in their place through roles and ritual practices, and in addition to developing a sense of shame, they will order themselves harmoniously."

18:37 | "If names be not correct, language is not in accordance with the truth of things. If language be not in accordance with the truth of things, affairs cannot be carried on to success. When affairs cannot be carried on to success, proprieties and music do not flourish." This was another one of Kǒngzǐ's passions. The *míng* (名) or name of something was extremely important.

19:01 | "The nobler type of man is broad-minded and not prejudiced. The inferior man is prejudiced and not broad-minded."

THE HISTORY OF CHINESE PHILOSOPHY
PART 4

19:10 | "When we see men of worth, we should think of equaling them; when we see men of a contrary character, we should turn inwards and examine ourselves."

19:19 | OK, let's pack up our rucksacks and call it a day. Next time we're all together we'll look at how Confucianism became what it ultimately became. In his own lifetime, Confucius was just another philosopher. But in death he attained immortality. That's all for next time in Part 5. This is Laszlo Montgomery signing off from Los Angeles, California. Thanks for listening and do consider joining me next time for another exciting episode of the China History Podcast.

The History of Chinese Philosophy Part 5

SUMMARY

Introduction to the School of Names, the Sophists, Deng Xi, Confucian classics become a pathway to a career in the government

TRANSCRIPT

00:00 | Greetings everybody, Laszlo Montgomery back with you again. This is Part 5 in a pretty long series covering the history of Chinese Philosophy. I thank you for fitting the CHP into your listening lineup.

00:15 | Before we get started I wanted to interject a quick word about the Jesuits and their role in bringing Chinese philosophy to the West. They learned early on about the nine classics that would later be called the *Sì Shū* and the *Wǔ Jīng*, *The Four Books* and *The Five Classics*. And the Jesuits learned early in their intel gathering mission, late 16th, early 17th centuries, that these books, like the Bible, were ancient and very sacred texts. And they poured all their industry, scholarship, religious devotion and intelligence into trying to translate them and figure these classics out.

THE HISTORY OF CHINESE PHILOSOPHY PART 5

00:54 They figured mastery of these classic texts might hold the key for the Jesuits in drawing parallels between Confucianism and their Catholic faith, and winning the Chinese over to their side using the good old comparison method, showing their potential converts: You see? You see? Same ideas!

01:15 Matteo Ricci got the translation process going and later in 1687, Jesuits Prospero Intorcetta together with Philippe Couplet published *The Life and Works of Confucius* in Latin. And this Latin version acted like a Rosetta Stone that allowed for further translations of Confucian and Daoist classics to be made into all the major languages of Europe. And good timing too. This all got rolling right on the eve of the Age of Enlightenment. All of those philosophic and literary greats of that age in Europe read and were familiar with Confucius through this work by Intorcetta and Couplet.

01:56 Thanks to the work of the Jesuits, during the 18th century European intellectuals got to feast on Chinese culture for the first time, and Kǒngfūzǐ — Confucius — he was an instant hit. There were others besides Kǒngzǐ walking the streets of China during this age of One Hundred Schools. One of the more amusing ones were all these so-called Sophists. Sophistry by definition is the use of fallacious arguments made with the intention of deceiving someone.

02:29 Language and writing had come far enough by the time of Kǒngzǐ that other clever thinkers emerged who were wizards at taking words and twisting their

THE HISTORY OF CHINESE PHILOSOPHY
PART 5

meaning and applying arguments that solved nothing and confounded everyone. This group of philosophers, of which there were many later on, were classified in the Han Dynasty as the School of Names. The *Míng Jiā*. Paradoxical conclusions were their stock in trade.

02:58 The most famous early example of these sophists would have to be Dèng Xī. China's first lawyer. He's called that, but that's not documented so far as I know. He's also credited with being China's Founding Father of Logic. He lived from more or less 545 to 501 BCE, which would make him contemporary with Confucius.

03:21 Back then you had people like Dèng Xī who, for a fee, defended clients in matters of civil dispute. He was a minor official in the state of Zhèng in modern-day Hénán. The *Zuǒ Zhuàn* points out that his claim to fame was a liberal penal code that he introduced.

03:39 Dèng Xī and these others who followed him always figured out ways to win for their clients in these many civil disputes. In Dèng Xī's day, as in our day as well, these lawyers, advocates or whatever you want to call them, came up with all kinds of clever ways to, well, ignore the spirit of the law and focus only instead on the names and actualities which could be picked apart and debated from a number of angles.

04:08 In his day, Dèng Xī was not regarded highly and was considered a troublemaker. One day he argued for one thing and the next day he'd take a contrarian position for another client, arguing both sides of the law. His

THE HISTORY OF CHINESE PHILOSOPHY
PART 5

cleverness later on put him on the wrong side of Duke Xiàn of Zhèng (鄭獻公) who ruled 513-501 BCE. The Duke had Dèng Xī executed.

04:33 A nice illustration of Dèng Xī at his best might be this signature story that comes to us straight from the *Lüshì Chūnqiū*, Master Lü's Spring and Autumn Annals.

04:44 It goes like this... Somebody was sailing their boat, making their way down the Wèi River when they came upon a man floating face down in the water. The captain of the boat went and fished the body out of the river. Inquiries were made and the one who found the body learned the family of the drowned man had quite a lot of money. So he asked for an exorbitant amount as a reward before he agreed to turn over the body. The grieving family at once sought out Dèng Xī for advice and the philosopher told them, "Don't worry, the price will come down. He can only sell the body to you. Who else is gonna want it?"

05:20 And then, wouldn't you know it, the same day later on, the man in possession of the unfortunate drowned victim also sought out Dèng Xī for advice on how to handle the situation. And Dèng Xī told him, "There's no need to negotiate! Hold your price. You're the only one he can recover the body from." Get the picture?

05:41 Dèng Xī and his ilk, they were just one of so many thinkers who exploded onto the scene in China mostly between the 6th to the 3rd centuries BCE. Confucius did not like these guys from the *Míng Jiā*, the School

THE HISTORY OF CHINESE PHILOSOPHY
PART 5

of Names. I already mentioned the story when he sentenced a man to death once for pulling these kinds of stunts, manipulating words to incite the masses.

06:08 Well, as we'll see later on, Confucianism all sounds nice and ideal but not everyone thought that way. And the Confucianists always had stiff competition with others who tried to muscle their way in to the pavilions of power. The Daoists and Buddhists most famously.

06:27 The Great Sage certainly got a heck of a drubbing during the Cultural Revolution. And starting in 1973, Kǒngzǐ got his very own political campaign: Pī Lín Pī Kǒng, Criticize Confucius and Lin Biao. That lasted three years.

06:42 And he also serves as one of the internationally recognized iconic symbols of Chinese culture.

06:49 Although it's called one of China's three religions, Confucianism is not a religion and has no deity. It's an entirely secular ideology. It's nothing like a religion in the sense of say, Christianity. Well, beginning in the Han, Kǒngzǐ was held up by some as a godhead type figure but, it wasn't like in the Judaeo-Christian sense.

07:13 The Shāng Dynasty deity was known as *shàngdì*. This was later replaced in the Zhou with the idea of *Tiān* or Heaven being the supreme deity who was moral force and dependent on humans to manifest its will.

07:29 As I mentioned a bit ago, from Confucianism developed this Chinese tradition of scholarship and love of learning.

THE HISTORY OF CHINESE PHILOSOPHY
PART 5

Later on, after the Hàn Dynasty is established, learning will become an entire industry that provided a conduit for people to better themselves and exercise that innate desire to achieve.

07:50   No greater glory could come to a common villager than to see their son pass the civil service exams and attain a rank in officialdom. Confucian learning became the greatest chance one had to go somewhere. Not in Confucius's lifetime, that is, but later on.

08:07   But as I indicated, the entire Confucian system and ethic had this built-in mechanism that kept women locked out of the whole system, and for this reason we can only speculate how much greatness and achievement was lost throughout the ages by only providing a path to success for 50% of the gene pool.

08:29   And many 19th and 20th century Chinese writers, thinkers and statesmen would later point to Confucianism as the guilty culprit for holding the nation back all these centuries. The ideology was accused of being too restricting, too inward-looking. It abhorred humankind's spirit of adventure. The ultimate goal seemed to be the never-ending quest for a kind of walled garden where all outside influences were kept where they belonged, on the outside. This was certainly true in the case of the decades following the Industrial Revolution.

09:06   And after the foreigners came in droves during the 19th century and ran roughshod over Chinese institutions

THE HISTORY OF CHINESE PHILOSOPHY
PART 5

and sensibilities, a lot of intellectuals pointed at Confucius and said... if it wasn't for him we wouldn't be in this situation.

09:23 You know, when you read all of these Confucian philosophers, Mèngzǐ, Xúnzǐ most notably, you can see all Master Kǒng called for besides reciprocity... do unto others as you'd have other do unto you... his main message was human decency, and he gave plenty of examples of what he meant. And as for rulers, what was so bad about rulers who were upright, moral, and engaged deliberately and with great sincerity, all the ceremonies of state and setting an example for the people under their rule?

09:56 Kǒngzǐ said, find this person, put him on the throne, and follow him. And because Kǒngzǐ showed six examples of such people, from Yáo all the way to the Duke of Zhōu, no one could say such a Sage-Ruler didn't exist.

10:11 And remember from last episode, the word Confucianism is a Western term. In Chinese, Confucianism is called called *Rújiā*. *Rú* meaning scholar. This school of thought encompasses more than just Confucius. It also includes all the commentaries everyone made who followed Master Kǒng. This is all grouped under the *Rújiā* or Ru School umbrella.

10:38 As we'll see in a later episode, with the passing of Confucius in 479 BCE, China will percolate on a high setting for 258 years before Qín Shǐhuáng vanquishes the last of the Warring States and established China's

53

THE HISTORY OF CHINESE PHILOSOPHY
PART 5

first imperial dynasty, the Qín. We'll look at those two and a half centuries later on and track the progress of Confucian thought as his disciples start to spin their magic.

11:07   We'll also examine the impact that the first Qín emperor had on Confucianism and everyone else who wasn't related to the state ideology of Legalism. We'll look at that too. So much more to go!

11:22   Coming up next, we'll look at more *Rú* School philosophers such as Mèngzǐ, Mòzǐ, Xúnzǐ, then see what happens to Chinese philosophy in the Qín and the Hàn Dynasties.

11:33   Okay, today's a short one. Class dismissed a little early. This is Laszlo Montgomery signing off from southern California. Thanks for listening and please consider coming back again next time for another exciting episode of the China History Podcast.

The History of Chinese Philosophy Part 6

THE TRANSCRIPTS

SUMMARY

More Ru School philosophers: Mozi, Yang Zhu, Mengzi

TRANSCRIPT

00:00 | Welcome back everyone. Laszlo Montgomery here with you once more. You're tuned in to the China History Podcast. Part 6 this time in our eighteen part series covering the history of Chinese philosophy.

00:15 | We're still in the Classical Period of Chinese philosophy. All the oldest and most sacred texts from the Shāng and Western Zhōu dynasties have been picked over the last few centuries. And then along came Confucius who saved the day when everyone was starting to ask, what in the heck do these old books have to do with anything to do with us in our day? Confucius re-introduced these traditions and shone a spotlight on these texts and taught that these words were still relevant.

00:46 | I want to say right now that although Confucius made a big splash late in his day and had attracted a lot of talented students, not everyone thought his teachings

THE HISTORY OF CHINESE PHILOSOPHY PART 6

were so great. One of those, credited with being the first important naysayer of Confucianism was Mòzǐ, also known as Mò Dí. He lived from 470 to 391 BCE, which means he was born about a decade after the death of Confucius, which also made Mòzǐ a contemporary of Socrates and Plato over in the West.

01:20 Like Confucius, Mòzǐ came from Lǔ from a non-aristocratic background. Like all these other philosophers he was an official. He served in the state of Sòng and had acquired quite a following, especially among the military men who were in the employ of various feudal lords. These were educated men like most knights-errant, but didn't have any aristocratic blood running through their veins. They were Mòzǐ's core followers and it's said they were a very organized militant lot, a very disciplined community, almost like a cult, with considerable geographic reach. Each group was overseen by a "Grand Master."

02:03 Mòzǐ was very big in his day, just as well known in the land as Confucius had been when he was still alive. And he had a solid reputation for being someone who practiced what he preached. As Confucius idealized Yáo, Mòzǐ's role model was Yǔ the Great, founder of the Xià Dynasty.

02:24 Mòzǐ's philosophy is called Mohism and his followers Mohists. They all hung their hat on several basic tenets taught in the fifty-three chapters that make up the work for which he is known, eponymously called *The Mòzǐ*.

THE HISTORY OF CHINESE PHILOSOPHY
PART 6

02:39 Master Mò said there was only one standard for everything. One objective moral standard above all, for right and for wrong. *The Mòzǐ* sums up Master Mò's teaching in Ten Theses. Like all these books, the author and the true creator of the content most likely not the same people.

03:04 The signature aspect of Mohism was Mòzǐ's concept of universal love or inclusive care. He taught that that was the answer. All people should love all people equally. That was the only way to solve the terrible problems plaguing society in these Warring States years.

03:22 And Mòzǐ was very anti-war and despite the militant background of his core followers, he said the only wars worth fighting were those defensive in nature. This quasi-religious, militant community of Mohists would sometimes go out and aid those states in dire need due to invasion by a bigger neighbor. They would provide all this expertise in defending against aggressors. Mohists embraced pacifism and for this reason, Mòzǐ's thought was the preferred choice of all pacifists.

03:57 "Make love not war" would have been Mòzǐ's slogan. You may consider all this anti-war, universal love thinking to be a good thing, but back people who thought this way were considered crackpots and way out on the political fringe. Some government officials even considered them anarchists. The Legalists, who we'll get to later, scoffed at Mòzǐ and assured him his vision of universal love was a pipe dream and that war would always end up being the final arbiter in political struggles.

 THE HISTORY OF CHINESE PHILOSOPHY
PART 6

04:30 | The Mohists really turned their noses up at Confucianism. And let me say the feelings were mutual. Mòzǐ taught that all of this teaching from these dusty old books just couldn't be more useless and impractical in their day. He described a Confucianist this way. They were "indolent and arrogant. Self-indulgent in drinking and eating and too lazy to work. He often suffers from hunger and cold and is in danger of freezing and starvation but lacks the ability to avert them. He behaves like a beggar, grasps food like a hamster, stares blankly like a he-goat and rises up like a pig. When the gentlemen all laugh at him, he becomes angry and exclaims, 'What do undisciplined men know about a good Confucian like me?' In spring and summer he begs for grain. After the 5 grains are gathered, he resorts to conducting funerals. When a death takes place in a rich family he will rejoice greatly, for it is his opportunity for clothing and food."

05:31 | Confucius lionized the old sages and the old ways. But Mòzǐ said they had no practical place in society and he sought to replace Confucian thought with something less complicated and more approachable.

05:44 | Mòzǐ said the Confucianists ruined the world in several ways: Firstly, Confucianists rejected that gods existed. Mòzǐ believed in gods, ghosts and spirits, and that *Tiān*, or Heaven, was the ultimate moral guide for humankind. He also said Confucianists were too strict with ceremonies and rituals. He noted, for example, the three-year period of mourning for one's parents as especially impractical, not to mention wasteful. Mòzǐ was also totally against the Confucian idea that

THE HISTORY OF CHINESE PHILOSOPHY
PART 6

everyone's fate was already pre-determined and that everyone should know their place! Mòzǐ said this kind of thinking was totally out of step with the times.

06:28 You see, the people who generally followed the Confucian way and those of the Mohist persuasion saw eye to eye on about as much as hardcore liberals and conservatives do today. For example, Mòzǐ's notion of universal all-embracing love was totally rejected by the Confucianists. Mòzǐ said love everyone equally. Confucianists thought this couldn't be more out of line. How could you love a stranger the same as a parent? Or a relative? Confucianism called for discriminating love. There were gradations, as far as who should matter more to you and of your relations who was due a greater degree of love.

07:08 "Mohists" were characterized by their commitment to these Ten Theses. Mòzǐ believed people naturally gravitated towards correct behavior. Selfishness was the root of all evil, and all-embracing love was the antidote to that. To ensure this kind of behavior, education was necessary to keep people ethical and moral.

07:31 A sampling of these Mohist Ten Theses, essentially promoted the following points of view: There should be a meritocracy. High-up positions should be open to everyone and should not be denied to people of low-birth who demonstrate the correct moral behavior and competence.

THE HISTORY OF CHINESE PHILOSOPHY
PART 6

07:49 Mòzǐ was against wasteful spending and called for moderation in all matters concerning luxuries and unnecessary expenditures, of which elaborate funerals, music and the arts were considered part of that category. Rituals too. Mòzǐ said that even though they didn't work and were too inflexible, they were still something positive for the way they brought families and all of society together in the shared participation.

08:15 Confucianists believed *Tiān,* or Heaven, was a moral force, but it did not get involved in humankind's affairs. Not so, said Mozi. Heaven rewarded the good and punished the bad.

08:28 And as far as his political philosophy was concerned, Mòzǐ said it was the state's role to define this standard. No surprise, the Mohists favored dictatorship over democracy. And when we get to Mèngzǐ in a moment, you'll see he's no fan of democracy either. Mòzǐ maintained that a dictatorship was the best way to set up a government, but that the dictator served at the will of the people and of Heaven. And the reason the whole Yellow and Wèi River Valley was awash in chaos was because of the dearth of capable rulers. A ruler's main job description was to spare the people from chaos and to govern with the idea of "impartial concern" for the welfare of the people. Impartial concern... everyone was the same.

09:17 Mohism, though it had a significant impact on early Chinese thought, didn't survive as a major school. It wasn't outright rejected. History books all seem to

THE HISTORY OF CHINESE PHILOSOPHY
PART 6

suggest that after the Qin Dynasty, Mohism died off, and its various philosophies absorbed by other schools. And why Mohism didn't survive beyond the Qín... we'll get to that in good time. There's nothing wrong with imagining the kind of utopian world that Mòzǐ envisioned. Like Confucius, he said it all began at the top with the leader. There had to be someone who was going to set a solemn example for the people, and from his example all of society will fall in line and everyone will help one another.

10:04 Without anyone looking, let's quietly and surreptitiously sneak out the back door here with Mohism and move on to another philosopher, thirty years younger than Mòzǐ but their lives had plenty of overlap.

10:18 I have to say of all the philosophers I picked over, from Yùzǐ to Wáng Yángmíng, this one intrigued me the most.

10:26 He lived from 440 to 360 BCE, again, Socrates-Plato times. He lived sort of in between Mòzǐ and Mèngzǐ. His name was Yáng Zhū. As I familiarized myself with Yáng Zhū I couldn't help marveling that he was teaching these words more than twenty-four centuries ago and the same words could have been said today in our day.

10:52 Yáng Zhū had an interesting and colorful way of looking at the world and how humankind should conduct themselves. First of all, wherever you read about Yáng Zhū, the caveat is always mentioned that says everything there is to know about him... slim pickins, baby, is all's it is, too. It was all said by his enemies, guys like Mèngzǐ.

THE HISTORY OF CHINESE PHILOSOPHY
PART 6

We only know of him through the words written about him by others, and no one was terribly complimentary.

11:23 Mòzǐ thought Confucius was wrong and Yáng Zhū thought both of those two were wrong. What did he say that was so eye-opening? Late in the 5th century BCE and into the 4th, Yáng Zhū summed his philosophy up in a way that reminded me of what Alvie Singer said in Annie Hall. I'm paraphrasing, but he compared life to the quality of the onboard meals you used to get on an airline. The food was terrible and such small portions, too, meaning life was hard and filled with misery and before you knew it, it was over all too soon. Therefore Yáng Zhū said it was humankind's sole purpose in life to counteract this potential misery by pursing pleasure and to enjoy a good time.

12:10 Yáng Zhū said there's no god, no afterlife, this is it. Once you're gone, you're gone and no matter how many monuments to your own personal glory you leave behind, you ain't gonna be there to hear people pass it on the street and talk about what a great person you were. Wise people will accept that they are like a tumbleweed, blown wherever the forces of nature take them.

12:33 Furthermore, he completely rejected Confucius, Mòzǐ and all these Rú scholars who taught about humans' inherent virtue and all-embracing love. Who were they kidding? Yáng Zhū even went as far as to say all this talk of ethics and how people should act is just a ruse or an excuse for the simple-minded to be manipulated by the educated elites.

THE HISTORY OF CHINESE PHILOSOPHY
PART 6

12:57 | Like Confucius, Yáng Zhū agreed that those were good times in the early Zhou. But Yáng Zhū parted ways with Master Kǒng when he said everything went south in China after all these philosophers burst onto the scene, wandering all over the country spreading their impractical theoretical nonsense.

13:18 | The marquee story from the life of Yáng Zhū that sort of encapsulates his view on how we should all live our lives, concerns the stories of Shùn, Yǔ and Confucius, as well as the two poster boys for evil sovereigns. I mentioned them previously? Jié and Zhòu Xīn, the final rulers of Xià and Shāng dynasties respectively.

13:39 | Yáng Zhū's reasoning was this. He said such morally standup guy's like Yáo and Shùn never had an easy day in their lives. In trying to achieve all they did in helping the people, life was a daily struggle with sadness and suffering. Yǔ the Great? His story was well known— to deal with the floods he was on the clock constantly, never taking a break, even forsaking his own family in his determination to tame the Yellow River floods. A lot of good his morals and virtuousness did for him and Shùn.

14:13 | As for Confucius? In the sage's own lifetime he was mocked, disrespected and ignored wherever he went. All these sages were perfect examples of virtue, yet look at how they struggled and never got to enjoy any of the fruits of their righteousness.

THE HISTORY OF CHINESE PHILOSOPHY
PART 6

14:32 Yáng Zhū pointed out that those men had been revered and hailed as perfect models for everyone to follow. But for what, asks Yáng? They're dead and gone and therefore oblivious to all the accolades that have been heaped on them since their passing.

14:48 Yáng Zhū then points to King Jié of Xià. He inherited wealth, got to be king, lived a life of pleasure and debauchery. Same with Zhòu Xīn. They did nothing except pursue a life of selfish pleasure. They died... we all die... and in death their venality and evil lives on. Always pointed to as a reminder to people about what happens when they act like they did. But, Yáng Zhū says, those two kings are as dead as Shùn and Confucius, and they have no idea that they have been turned into roles models for licentiousness and evil.

15:25 Who had the better life in the end? Jié and Zhòu Xīn, or the paragons of virtue who are held up to all people as the models for how we should think and conduct ourselves? Yáng Zhū said people should just act naturally, in your own self-interest and don't blindly follow these social niceties. Do what's best for you. These rituals, traditions, beliefs and listening to these sages from five hundred years ago... feh! It ain't gonna help you. If you see something, take it if it's going to make you happy, or give you pleasure.

16:00 Thankfully for Kǒngzǐ, he did not live to hear Yáng Zhū expound on this rather hedonistic philosophy. Hedonism: that's the pursuit of pleasure and happiness. Pleasure is the highest good. This was epicureanism's embarrassing

64

THE HISTORY OF CHINESE PHILOSOPHY
PART 6

relative. What a world it would be if we all thought like Yáng Zhū. But from a Daoist perspective... he wasn't so bad. If self-preservation was the innate way for humans to act, then why go against what only came natural.

16:34 Confucius didn't live to hear Yáng Zhū, but Mèngzǐ did. And there's this famous snippet from the Mengzi where he laments that, "The words of Yáng Zhū and Mò Dí fill the world. If you listen to people's discourses about it, you will find that they have adopted the views of one or the other. Now Yang's principle is "Each for himself" — which does not acknowledge the claims of the sovereign. Mò's principle is, "To love all equally" — which does not acknowledge the peculiar affection due to a father. To acknowledge neither king nor father is to be in the state of a beast. If their principles are not stopped, and the principles of Confucius set forth, their perverse speaking will delude the people, and stop up the path of benevolence and righteousness. I am alarmed by these things, and address myself to the defense of the doctrines of the former sages, and to oppose Yáng and Mò. I drive away their licentious expressions, so that such perverse speakers may not be able to show themselves. When sages shall rise up again, they will not change my words." Mèngzǐ, Ladies and Gentlemen. We'll be getting to him in a minute.

17:50 Mèngzǐ wasn't the only 4th century BCE philosopher to heavily diss Yang Zhu. Hán Fēi, Lǐ Sī and others rejected this thought. But as I said before I started discussing about Yáng Zhū, all we know about him is what other's wrote about him. None of his work survives. Like Yùzǐ

65

THE HISTORY OF CHINESE PHILOSOPHY
PART 6

	from Part 1 and many others throughout history, we only know of them and can read of their work only those bits that later writers wrote and what fate allowed to survive into our time.
18:25	So Yang Zhu passed away in 360 BCE. Let's look at Confucianism after Confucius. The two greatest interpreters of Confucius during the Classical period were Mèngzǐ and Xúnzǐ. Let's focus on Master Mèng first.
18:43	Mèngzǐ, born Mèng Kē, came from the state of Zōu. Zōu bordered Lǔ to the south and today would be part of southern Shandong. He lived from 372 to 289 BCE, roughly the time of Aristotle in Greece and young Alexander the Great. We're in the Warring States Period in China still and as the countdown to 221 BCE gets closer, the times just keep getting worse.
19:11	Some older Chinese around the world who went to a traditional Chinese school might remember the stories of Mengzi's mother pounded into them when they were young. Mèngzǐ's mother, Mèng Mǔ, she was put up on the highest possible pedestal and was forever pointed to as a living representation of virtue and what it means, in the traditional sense, to be the perfect mother. She was perhaps China's first Tiger Mom. Lots of stories featuring Mengzi's mother, and a few good *chengyu* also. In fact, Mèngzǐ in general. He appeared in more Chinese Sayings than almost anyone.

THE HISTORY OF CHINESE PHILOSOPHY
PART 6

19:51 This is not a character that was unique to Mèng Mǔ. There were other women who were held up and praised as this idealized woman, who is also a mother, who puts everyone else's needs and interests before themselves, who, through their tears, sacrifice and hardships clears the path for her children to be good and decent and to go on and thrive. That's nothing new. In Rome, for example, we can point to Cornelia Africana, mother of Tiberius and Gaius. Cornelia Africana isn't a household name, but when history buffs hear about the so-called "Mother of the Gracchi", they know what those four words signify.

20:35 Oppressed Chinese women throughout the centuries, I guess, have Mèngzǐ's mother to thank for making as big a deal as she did about the Three Obediences. These Three Obediences didn't necessarily enslave Chinese women for two thousand years, but let's say it contributed no small amount to the limiting the career options that women had.

20:58 Yeah, we have Mèng Mǔ who uttered the words, "It does not belong to a woman to determine anything for herself, but she is subject to the rule of the Three Obediences. When young, she has to obey her parents; when married, she has to obey her husband; when a widow, she has to obey her son."

21:21 This was known as the Sān Cóng Sì Dé. The Three Obediences and the Four Virtues. Not just these three obediences to the men in their life. Women had to maintain these four virtues, these *sì dé* — morality, *dé*;

67

THE HISTORY OF CHINESE PHILOSOPHY
PART 6

physical charm, *róng*; propriety in speech, *yán*; and efficiency in needlework, *gōng*.

21:44 Mengzi's mother, a tough act to follow. And on that note, let's take a break and reconvene in the next episode where you can be sure we will examine the life, deeds and philosophical thought of Mengzi. After Confucius himself, Mengzi or Mencius, he's the biggest thing there is in Confucian philosophy. I might be able to squeeze Xúnzǐ in too. We'll see. So, I look forward to seeing you then.

22:09 Thanks one more time. This is Laszlo Montgomery, signing off from the City of Night, inviting you back next time for another exciting episode of the China History Podcast.

 The History of Chinese Philosophy Part 7

THE TRANSCRIPTS

SUMMARY

More about Mengzi and introducing Xunzi

TRANSCRIPT

00:00 | Welcome back all CHP listeners from all across the universe! Laszlo Montgomery back with more Chinese Philosophy, just as the title of the episode advertises. Thanks for listening to the China History Podcast. As I promised you last time, we're going to continue on with more Rú School philosophy and look at Mèngzǐ, also known by his Latinized name of Mencius.

00:25 | I finished off last episode speaking about Mengzi's mother and her role in shaping the Confucianist demands that women had to put up with. She's always held up as this shining example of the perfectly devoted mother.

00:39 | Let me start with the most famous Mèngzǐ story from his early years that gave us one of the most famous Chinese Sayings or *chéngyǔ*. This was Mèng Mǔ Sān Qiān, which translates to 'Mèngzǐ's Mother moves three times'. It

THE HISTORY OF CHINESE PHILOSOPHY
PART 7

was just the two of them, growing up. No father. Mèng Mǔ, Mengzi's mother, settled down first at a shack near a cemetery and noticed right away little Mengzi engaging in pretend ceremonies for the dead. So she didn't like to see that, and decided to pick up and move to a place near a thriving market town. But before long, she saw her son acting like some merchant and talking about money all the time. So, she pulled up stakes again and found a third place that had a school as its closest landmark. And when Mèngzǐ's mother saw her son trying to learn and show some manners and decency, she decided she had finally found the right place.

01:41 Mèng Mǔ Sān Qiān. Yeah, this whole idea of Chinese mothers who want the best education for their children... trust me that didn't start with Amy Chua. It went back at least as far as Mèng Mǔ, the mother of Mèngzǐ. And although it went against the Confucian idea of simplicity and frugality, when Mèngzǐ's mother passed, her filial son gave her one heck of a glorious well-deserved send-off, one that I'm willing to bet Mòzǐ wouldn't have approved of.

02:14 Master Kǒng... Confucius...simply resting on his own laurels, most likely today would not be gracing the name of all these hundreds of Confucius Institutes around the world. We remember Confucius because he received a little help along the way. First from his immediate disciples and then from Mèngzǐ, followed by Xúnzǐ and then I guess by Dǒng Zhòngshū, but let's not get too ahead of ourselves. They were the first ones to begin the process of interpreting what it was Confucius

THE HISTORY OF CHINESE PHILOSOPHY
PART 7

02:52 taught when he was alive. Remember Kǒngfūzǐ didn't write anything down.

Mèngzǐ was born after Confucius, who had already been gone for a hundred and seven years. I mentioned at the outset, he supposedly studied under Confucius's grandson Zǐ Sī. The first thing Mengzi did when he left the nest was to hang out his own shingle and open up a school. Having studied under someone like Zǐ Sī was like bragging you had a Harvard or Yale degree. So Mèngzǐ was able to attract a lot of students, many who went on to great things in the government and civil service.

03:23 Mèngzǐ was no different from any of these philosophers anxious to advise rulers on how to rule their state, and how to bring about the greatest amount of prosperity, peace, stability and happiness for the people. From about 323 to 314 BCE Mèngzǐ did his wandering. He went to Qí first and found employment with the ruler, Qí Xuān Gōng, Duke Xuān of Qí. He accepted an honorary post and refused any salary. But in advising Duke Xuān, Mèngzǐ soon figured out he wasn't being taken seriously.

04:01 So Mèngzǐ moved on, but Duke Xuān of Qí called him back. Mèngzǐ soon saw that it was futile trying to turn this militant king into a benevolent and virtuous leader. This Duke Xuān had all kinds of designs on other states and was looking to acquire some kingdoms.

04:22 Mèngzǐ implored him to make peace, not war, and to rule his people with benevolence and morality and to serve as a model for his people. Then, not only his

THE HISTORY OF CHINESE PHILOSOPHY
PART 7

subjects in Qí would revere him, but others would flock to Qi as well just to call him their ruler.

04:40 It's not surprising that Mengzi ultimately got canned by Qí Xuān Gōng. This pugnacious ruler didn't like Mèngzǐ's pacifism. So like all these itinerant philosophers, Mèngzǐ moved on to the next place, always vigilant for that philosopher-king in the rough who only needed Mèngzǐ's finishing touches to turn him into the virtuous Zhou Dynasty founder King Wén re-born. Like Confucius, and no doubt many a philosopher, Mèngzǐ searched in vain. In the end, he just settled down and returned to teaching.

05:17 Besides teaching, he wrote about all the rulers he had rubbed elbows with during his travels and discussed the conversations he had with them. These dialogs were all part of the book that bears his name, the Mèngzǐ. It's one of the Classics. Some say this was one of those ancient works that was actually written by the alleged author, rather than his disciples or those who came after him. But... 300 BCE... can't say for sure.

05:45 Mèngzǐ taught the original goodness of human nature. Innately, humans were good. He called it *xìng shàn*. Like Aristotle and later John Locke's tabula rasa, people were born good. They are made bad thanks to poor leadership setting a bad example. And this bad example set by others impacted people who didn't know any better. Mèngzǐ said either philosophers must become kings or kings must become philosophers.

72

THE HISTORY OF CHINESE PHILOSOPHY PART 7

06:17 | Mengzi's philosophy claims that human beings have four beginnings. Here's how he put them. "The feeling of commiseration is the beginning of human heartedness. The feeling of shame and dislike is the beginning of righteousness. The feeling of modesty and yielding is the beginning of propriety. The sense of right and wrong is the beginning of wisdom."

06:43 | These Four Beginnings are also called the Four Virtues. Some in the West have referred to them as Mengzi's Four Cardinal Virtues. All people are born with them, these innate ethical predispositions. And throughout one's life it was essential to nurture and develop these four virtues so that in time they will become the Four Constant Virtues. By further developing the Four Constant Virtues, one can achieve sage-hood.

07:14 | So these Four virtuous qualities, benevolence, righteousness, propriety, and wisdom, we all have it but if you don't use it you will lose it. Mèngzǐ would tell you, of the four virtues, benevolence and righteousness were the two most important.

07:31 | So you can see why Mèngzǐ would completely reject someone like Yáng Zhū. Mèngzǐ was an optimist. He said it was a moral universe that humans inhabited and it all began at the top with a virtuous ruler who ruled through benevolence and set an example for uprightness and propriety for all his subjects to see.

07:53 | Sure, people cared about many of these pleasures itemized by Yáng Zhū. But Mèngzǐ said people were

THE HISTORY OF CHINESE PHILOSOPHY
PART 7

also ethical and knew what the right thing to do was.

08:03 Confucius put his focus on the individual and to a lesser extent on the state. Mèngzǐ's focus was the state. It all began with the ruler. And not only that. On the one hand, Mèngzǐ taught what the qualities that a ruler must have and exhibit. He also was very Jeffersonian in his belief that if rulers become inept, or any Jié's or Zhòu Xīn's appear on the scene, the people have the right to remove them, even kill him if it comes to that. These were very radical ideas for their time.

08:37 And because Mèngzǐ was well-known for this line of political philosophy, the Hóngwǔ Emperor, after he founded the Ming Dynasty in 1368, will ban him, demoting Mèngzǐ in the Confucian Temple. Yeah, early Míng, Mèngzǐ will have to lay low and remain in the doldrums until he makes a comeback. The early Míng emperors didn't like that Jeffersonian belief about the tree of liberty needing to be refreshed with the blood of patriots and tyrants every so often.

09:07 And as far as democracy goes and that whole notion of government of the people and by the people, Mengzi didn't go for that. He thought that monarchy was the only way to go. Why was that? He said in order for the system to work, all people had to be educated. If not, the system breaks down and there is chaos. Nothing out-trumps a benevolent and virtuous ruler leading by example. That's all it takes, one single philosopher king.

THE HISTORY OF CHINESE PHILOSOPHY
PART 7

09:39 | In fact, Mèngzǐ said there were two kinds of rulers. One was a *wáng* and one was a *bà*. A *wáng* rules by virtue and benevolence... basically how Confucius thought they should conduct themselves. *Wáng* means king. And *bà*... they rule by force. This would be like a feudal lord or military hegemon. Mèngzǐ was vehemently anti-war, he thought it was a crime and nothing good ever came of it. And certainly no one deserved to be lionized for their military achievements.

10:14 | As far as Mòzǐ was concerned, Mèngzǐ's major beef with him was that impartial caring thing. To Mèngzǐ, putting the extent of your total caring on a stranger the same way you would your own flesh and blood, let alone your parents...Pshaw! as Tom Sawyer woulda said.

10:32 | Mèngzǐ was the shining star of the idealistic wing of Confucianism. He had a lot of detractors. For one thing, Mengzi's thought was criticized by many for being artificial. People weren't born good, they had to work hard to be good. All this morality and propriety...it was all artificial and forced, not the natural way people acted.

10:57 | Let's close things out with Xúnzǐ. He was another major Confucianist but he didn't see eye to eye with everything Mèngzǐ said, especially about the innate goodness of human nature.

11:10 | Everyone knows Confucius. Everyone knows Mencius. How come Xúnzǐ didn't get a Latinized name? Maybe for this reason. He remains in the shadow of his two more famous predecessors.

THE HISTORY OF CHINESE PHILOSOPHY
PART 7

11:23 | Xúnzǐ's name was Xún Kuàng. He was a native of Zhào State but he made his name in Qí. He lived from 313 to 238 BCE, passing away seventeen years before Qín Shǐhuáng enjoyed the sweet smell of success in 221 BCE. So we can say he lived during the last decades of the Warring States Period. He was twenty-four when Mengzi died. But let me say there's quite a disparity in Xúnzǐ's dates as far as when historians say he actually lived and died.

11:58 | Like Mèngzǐ, Kǒngzǐ and others, Xúnzǐ did his tour of the realm as well, calling on rulers, princes and anyone in authority who would see him. Like those other great thinkers, Xúnzǐ would try to proffer his advice to those in power on the best ways to end the misery, violence and bloodletting of the Eastern Zhōu Warring States Period. But this philosopher's renown ended up being due to his stature at the Jìxià Academy.

12:30 | Xúnzǐ left his mark as one of the greatest philosophers to come out of this *Jìxià Xué Gōng*. This institution was set up in 318 BCE by, yes, Duke Xuān of Qí, *Qí Xuān Gōng*. One and the same as the ruler who wasted Mengzi's time. Yeah, he didn't listen to Mengzi but he did act as the benefactor of this school that attracted *la crème de la crème* of pre-Qín Dynasty teachers and philosophers.

13:00 | This was China's first Think Tank. There, the most brilliant and innovative minds in what comprised China that far back, come together, to teach, to learn, to loaf, drink tea, complain and argue all their respective schools of thought.

THE HISTORY OF CHINESE PHILOSOPHY
PART 7

13:18 Let's look at Xúnzǐ, and particularly through the prism of Mèngzǐ, since he's so fresh in our minds right now. They were both dyed-in-the-wool Confucianists but they didn't see eye to eye on a few key points.

13:32 What do we most remember Xúnzǐ for? Well, Lǎozǐ's name is mentioned for the first time in Xúnzǐ's work. Do you remember how Mèngzǐ said people, by nature, are born good? They're corrupted by all the blowback from having an inferior ruler. Mengzi maintained one had to focus and work deliberately to retain their innate goodness.

13:54 Well, Xúnzǐ... He said just the opposite, and in this respect he was in lockstep with Yáng Zhū. Xúnzǐ said human nature was innately bad. Human nature's natural inclination is to be selfish and look out for number one first and foremost. Innately people are in a sense, evil and self-centered and from that base, he taught his philosophy.

14:20 After all, if people were as Mengzi said, innately good, then who would need these sage kings and all these boring rituals and strict etiquette?

14:30 Xúnzǐ said, don't blame the government for all the ills in society. They have nothing to do with the people's innate goodness. It was up to the people to become good. And this was attained by basically following Confucian thought. This included the rituals and ceremonies. Xúnzǐ said even though most everyone was lip synching and artificially embracing Confucianism and rituals

THE HISTORY OF CHINESE PHILOSOPHY
PART 7

in their daily lives, it was important to the masses of people. Especially at the state level, having rulers carry out these elaborate rituals, no matter to Heaven or to ancient ancestors. They were carrying out something that was very important to the people who were unable to express these emotions and feelings in this kind of way. It united ruler and people. Whether it worked or not was immaterial.

15:22 Xúnzǐ had written about how these rituals bound society as one but, he said, "You pray for rain and it rains. Why? For no particular reason, I say. It is just as though you had not prayed for rain and it rained anyway."

15:40 But Xúnzǐ and Mengzi agreed on the idea that no matter born good or born evil, a person can become a sage. And to do this one needed to be disciplined and live their life in the most deliberate way, not only talking the talk. Both philosophers believed the transformative powers of Confucian sincerity, ritual and learning could turn someone into a sage and keep society on an even keel.

16:09 As for Mengzi's Four Virtues... Four Beginnings that human nature contained... Not so, said Xúnzǐ. No Four Virtues, but there WAS one thing that humans were born with that was the key to rising above their innate desires for personal profit and sensual pleasures, and that was intelligence. Intelligence is the key to becoming good.

16:34 The learning which is the natural by-product of intelligence, should be used by the people to reform their innate unsavory human nature. It would reform

THE HISTORY OF CHINESE PHILOSOPHY
PART 7

them, and transform them. Mengzi said all this learning was like ongoing education for what was already good within you.

16:53 Mengzi said becoming a Yáo or a Shùn was possible because people were born good. And if one could sustain this goodness throughout their life they might one day look upon Yao and Shun as equals. Xúnzǐ said nobody's born a Yáo. But people had intelligence, and if they used this, they could one day become a Yáo.

17:15 I read that of this school of Rú Philosophy, Confucius, all his disciples and their disciples, Mengzi, Xunzi... that Mengzi is considered the left wing of the ideology and Xúnzǐ the right wing.

17:32 All of Xúnzǐ's philosophy is contained in... I know... you guessed it... another work named after the author, *The Xúnzǐ*. This thirty-two chapter work has a somewhat unique claim to fame amongst the classics. It's said that at least twenty-five of the chapters were actually written by Xúnzǐ. And a lot of it was written in essay style, and very nicely too. Works attributed to Mengzi and Kongzi were usually written in dialogue form.

18:02 What Xúnzǐ did that separated himself from Mèngzǐ was to look at the times they lived in and synthesized other elements of thought that weren't necessarily Confucian in their origin. He picked around other schools of thought for ideas that could be copied and pasted onto Confucianism. In addition to Confucian ethics, he studied how others viewed ethics. He also gathered

THE HISTORY OF CHINESE PHILOSOPHY
PART 7

aspects of metaphysics, political theory, philosophy of language and education, whatever was applicable to Confucianism and enhanced it as an ideology.

18:39   The Confucian Dào is not the same as the Lǎozǐ-Zhuāngzǐ Dào. Mèngzǐ's Dào was more in line with the Daoists in that the Dao was the Way of Heaven and nature. Xúnzǐ's Dao focused on humanity. This Dao, or Way, was the Dao of human behavior, the way one is supposed to act in maintaining a harmonious society. Xúnzǐ said nature is nature and Heaven is Heaven and nothing can change that. It's a waste of time to speculate about it. Xúnzǐ's philosophy was closer to home, concerned only with the practical aspects of humanity, the human Way, the human Dao, a Way of behaving.

19:24   Okay, we will most certainly come back to Xunzi later on. I wanted to introduce him to you and I hope you'll remember him. Kǒngzǐ, Mèngzǐ, Xúnzǐ. These were the three giants of the pre-Qin Dynasty Rú School of Philosophy.

19:40   I didn't say this, but Xúnzǐ is famous for one other thing. And during the Qin Dynasty this was a good thing! But in the Han Dynasty, it wasn't. Xúnzǐ had two famous students when he was teaching at the Jìxià Academy in Qí state. These were Hán Fēi and Lǐ Sī. It was the teaching of these two shining stars of Xúnzǐ, Hán Fēi and Lǐ Sī, who provided all the requisite ideology that Qín Shǐhuáng needed to rule his empire. All for next time.

THE HISTORY OF CHINESE PHILOSOPHY
PART 7

20:15 | So let's close things out and bring down the curtains. Legalism is an ancient philosophy that gets discussed quite a bit in the 2020s with respect to the merits of what it espouses. So, this one you probably won't wanna miss. Until that time, me little beauties, this is Laszlo Montgomery signing off from Los Angeles, as usual. Thanks for listening and I'll see you next time with another exciting episode of the China History Podcast.

The History of Chinese Philosophy Part 8

THE TRANSCRIPTS

SUMMARY

Legalism during the Qin, Shang Yang, Shen Buhai, Han Fei, Li Si

TRANSCRIPT

00:00 Welcome back, my friends, to the show that never ends, Laszlo Montgomery here. Thanks for tuning in to the China History Podcast. Almost but not quite halfway through with this epic series introducing everything about Chinese Philosophy that you'd need to know, if you ever participate in a game show where the category was Chinese Philosophers.

00:22 Here I'm going to introduce Xúnzǐ's other claim to fame, namely, his two famous students.

00:28 Today in this episode we're going to look at Legalism and how it became the ideology embraced by the First Qin Emperor, and I guess you can say a lot of emperors who followed as well.

THE HISTORY OF CHINESE PHILOSOPHY
PART 8

00:39 Let's first talk about Hán Fēi and Lǐ Sī. Master Hán Fēi, of course famous for the *Hán Fēi Zǐ*, the fifty-five chapter book that bears his name. And Lǐ Sī, the Machiavellian right-hand man to the first emperor and also a giant in Chinese culture too. The small seal script, and other things. Both of these luminaries from Chinese history studied at the Jìxià Academy in Qí under Xúnzǐ.

01:09 Xúnzǐ died in 238 BCE. The final and longest-reigning Zhou Dynasty King, King Nǎn was deposed in 256 BCE, in Xúnzǐ's lifetime. Then from 259 to 221 BCE, Qín Shǐhuáng will do his thing and finish up his conquest of all the Warring States. And after his annexation of the once unstoppable Qí State, there will be a unified Chinese country with an emperor ruling over a large land mass, for the first time.

01:46 But remember, geographically this Chinese empire may have been a new polity, but the culture contained within this empire was already a good two thousand years old.

01:57 The Zhou Dynasty may have fallen in 256 BCE, but the decline really began in the 8th century BCE. So it's safe to say for something like five hundred years in China, people had been living in a society where there was no strong central authority and you never knew when some neighboring state might invade your homeland.

02:20 Five hundred years ago for us was the year 1521, so stop and think about living in a place for more than fifty generations where all you knew was the specter of war... That's a long time.

THE HISTORY OF CHINESE PHILOSOPHY
PART 8

02:33 Guǎn Zhòng primed the pump for Confucius. And it was Shāng Yāng as well as Shēn Bùhài and Shèn Dào... they did the same for Hán Fēi and Lǐ Sī. Shāng Yāng, 390 to 338 BCE, was a contemporary of Mèngzǐ and Zhuāngzǐ. He was a nobleman who served as an advisor to Duke Xiào of Qín. Shāng Yāng introduced reforms in Qín that greatly enhanced the power and reach of the central authority. These reforms called for strict laws and severe punishments that, in theory, would deter people from deviating from the Party Line, so to speak.

03:13 Reforms were also carried out in trade and commerce as well and on controlling the movements of the people. All of Shāng Yāng's main ideas were written into the Book of Lord Shang... yeah, you guessed right... known as the Shāngzǐ, or the Shāng Jūn Shū. It wasn't what you would call Legalism. But the Shāngzǐ surely gave Hán Fēi and Lǐ Sī food for thought.

03:37 Shēn Bùhài is quite an interesting historic figure. Aside from his work in Legalist thought and its impact on Hán Fēi and the Legalism adopted by the Qin, Shēn Bùhài is known as one of the creators of the Chinese administrative system. The Legalists are credited with discovering and implementing the so-called imperial administrative system that lasted for two thousand years. Well, Shēn Bùhài... not an A-Lister, I can tell you that... his contribution in actually designing the system was profound, especially with respect to establishing a meritocratic system. This will later lead to the subsequent Civil Service Exams.

THE HISTORY OF CHINESE PHILOSOPHY
PART 8

04:23 | Shēn Bùhài was one of the first to say, screw virtue, give me leaders who know how to do their job.

04:31 | Hán Fēi and Lǐ Sī were born in the same year, 280 BCE. Hán Fēi came from Hán State. Ancient Hán State was quite small, and surrounded by Chǔ, Qín and Wèi. Talk about two rocks and a hard place! Hán today would be spread out over portions of Shanxi and Henan. It's said Hán Fēi became so disgusted with the degradation in the Hán rulers leadership abilities he got fed up and bolted. As I said, he later ended up studying at the Jìxià Academy under Xúnzǐ. And there he met Lǐ Sī.

05:10 | As Sīmǎ Qiān tells it, Hán Fēi had a stutter which limited his options as far as becoming an orator or teacher went. Therefore Hán Fēi put all his talents into writing. And of all the Chinese classics, I have it on good authority, the Hán Fēizǐ is the most elegantly written.

05:32 | One day, Hán Fēi received a letter from his old schoolmate Lǐ Sī. Lǐ Sī knew the prime minister to Yíng Zhèng, King of Qín. This prime minister was of course Lǚ Bùwéi who we all know, after helping his king Yíng Zhèng make it to the top, is going to come to a bad end. Lǚ Bùwéi was Lǐ Sī's connection at the royal palace.

05:56 | Lǐ Sī became a very close advisor to the future first emperor of China. And he remembered his old classmate back at the Jìxià Academy days and called him out to Qin to help him do all these great things. So off to Qín Hán Fēi went, and to say that he became a big hit there is quite the understatement.

86

THE HISTORY OF CHINESE PHILOSOPHY
PART 8

06:17 | Hán Fēi, by this time in his career, had figured people out. Like his teacher Xúnzǐ, he agreed... people, they ain't no good. Han Fei wrote, "The natural aspirations of the people are such that they all move toward security and benefit and avoid danger and poverty, public spirited people are few while private minded people are numerous." And further to this, Han Fei did not believe education or purposeful self-cultivation worked either. Not on a practical level. Han Fei's famous words, "People go for benefits as water flows downwards."

07:00 | So where do we go from the viewpoint that people ain't no good from the start? That sure is an uphill climb. Hán Fēi said people were like wood. He said, look at such a commonplace plentiful thing as an arrow. Don't we use the term straight as an arrow? Well you can't find wood that's straight in nature. You have to condition it and put it through a process to make that arrow straight. You just can't pick a branch off a tree and stick an arrowhead on the end. Han Fei said people were the same way.

07:33 | He parted ways with Confucius, Mengzi, Xunzi and all those Rú School philosophers. He said yeah yeah yeah, all these traditions, rituals, learning and etiquette are all nice to follow and maybe they make some people good. But it's just not practical. How many Confucians can you find out there who are truly capable to administer the country? The Great Sage only had seventy-seven disciples. That's not enough firepower to make a difference on a national scale.

THE HISTORY OF CHINESE PHILOSOPHY
PART 8

08:06 | Hán Fēi said there's nothing that can beat the effectiveness of the carrot and the stick. If you want an efficiently run government you must establish a true meritocracy where only the most talented will rise. Their virtue or other Confucian qualities are subordinate to the quality of the job they perform.

08:29 | Furthermore, the system ran on the principle that everyone along the chain of command from the highest official down to the village peasant, had something in it for them if they did well, and followed the rules.

08:43 | These Rú School philosophers particularly lionized the ancients and pointed to them as the examples to follow. Hán Fēi said those guys are all dead and gone and times have changed drastically since they walked the earth.

08:58 | Like most of the philosophers of the Zhou era, he believed the answer to creating a rich and prosperous society all began with the central authority. The king, for example. The military is top rate and the peasants always productive. Hán Fēi teaches there are five tools at the ruler's disposal. First is the power of his position. There are also administrative methods. Third is the law. Fourth are the Two Handles, and Fifth is the Way, or Dao, of the Ruler.

09:39 | The Two Handles. What are those? Han Fei calls these the two things that the ruler and only the ruler, with no exceptions, can control. This is the authority to divvy out rewards and punishment. If he allowed one of his ministers to wield this power on his behalf, Han Fei said,

THE HISTORY OF CHINESE PHILOSOPHY
PART 8

the people would no longer fear the king and would instead try to curry favor and avoid getting on the bad side of the one who held this authority. Only the ruler touched those so-called two handles of government.

10:15 Han Fei said Legalism worked this way: first you put into place a legal system and make sure everyone from the bottom up all understood it. Everyone knew what lines not to cross and what was expected from them. Is a person good? Are they bad? What was a person's innate nature? Han Fei said it didn't matter. That wasn't going to do anything, and besides was entirely impractical, too theoretical. Virtue was nice, but laws were what kept people in order. People didn't have to be good, but they were not allowed to be bad. Legalism didn't seek to improve people, it was all just about managing them.

10:58 Legalism wasn't just all about laws. It was both an ideology, administrative and a political system all rolled up into one.

11:09 And the ruler need not be a sage. Their power was derived through their authority, not their virtue and benevolence. Just as Shēn Bùhài had said in the mid-4th century BCE. The kings used the Dao of their position, acting like a ruler is supposed to act, managing their officials and ministers, saying little but controlling everything.

11:34 Because people are born selfish, the ruler appeals to the self-serving nature of people and hangs rewards and profit in front of them as encouragement to do well. And

THE HISTORY OF CHINESE PHILOSOPHY
PART 8

	for those who break the laws, no matter who you were, everyone paid equally.
11:52	Hán Fēi believed this system was foolproof because it appealed to the natural evilness of human nature. All people had to do was act naturally. And as long as the laws are enforced, in time everything will become second nature to everyone. So you can see how something like this, and it was very detailed, how it would appeal to a ruler. Confucianists failed to offer a solution. Their thought was too theoretical. If it only worked, it would be great, but it didn't. Legalism was the practical solution. Idealism vs Realism.
12:28	That's Legalism in a peanut shell… People by nature are not, as Mèngzǐ would have you believe, innately good. They are the opposite, and for this reason you have to build a sociopolitical system that recognizes these selfish interests that people have. If people see they can attain pleasure and avoid pain by acting a certain way, that's all that matters.
12:52	This idea had profound political ramifications. The ruler, through their intrinsic power over the two handles, crafted a very tight, well-controlled administrative bureaucracy. If you showed quantifiable results, you worked your way up. If you were bad at your job, you went nowhere, or worse.
13:14	Legalism's contribution to the future growth of China was in part due to its role in building the superstructure of the imperial bureaucracy. The Qin Dynasty didn't last

THE HISTORY OF CHINESE PHILOSOPHY PART 8

13:38 too long, but this way of organizing the government did… a real long time. Again, Shēn Bùhài. He is the unsung hero of this achievement.

13:38 Hán Fēizǐ, as I mentioned earlier, became the darling of the Qin court. His elegant and forceful writing, where he so exquisitely synthesized the Legalist writings of those who came before him, and took all these ideas and injected his thought that was specifically relevant to those late 3rd century BCE times. He became everyone's favorite. And that's when Lǐ Sī decided to turn on his old Jìxià Academy classmate.

14:09 Fearing his star might possibly be eclipsed by Hán Fēi, Lǐ Sī began to suspect him and become jealous of all this attention he was getting, especially at the royal court. So one day in 233 BCE, Lǐ Sī whispered to the king, Yíng Zhèng, that Hán Fēi couldn't be trusted, and he gave a bunch of reasons. The future first emperor, a man known for his paranoia, thereupon ordered Hán Fēi to be locked up in prison.

14:41 Then, as the story goes, Lǐ Sī was so worried that King Yíng Zhèng would change his mind, he sent poison to Hán Fēi in his jail cell and suggested he better take this painless way out rather than suffer what the king had in store for him.

14:56 Then sure enough, just as Lǐ Sī feared, the king had a change of mind about the matter and called for Hán Fēi to be released. But too late. Hán Fēi had already been tricked into consuming the poison. A Double betrayal by

THE HISTORY OF CHINESE PHILOSOPHY
PART 8

Lǐ Sī, but he'll get his later on.

15:15 So Hán Fēi never lived to see the great success his ideology became during that rigid and severe decade of the Qin Dynasty. The success of Legalism as the state ideology didn't win any popularity contests. Once Qín Shǐhuáng sealed his victory in 221 BCE, a few things are going to happen that will blow a little wind in the sails of Legalism.

15:44 In addition to building the Great Wall and his magnificent tomb, the First Qin Emperor had a lot of big ideas about the direction he wanted to take China. From the moment the Qin emperor declared victory, he faced his detractors. The loudest voices were all coming from many of these philosophers. They acted in a way like the conscience of the day. They spoke out, no doubt quite eloquently, against some of the policies called for by the Qín emperor.

16:16 Well, Lǐ Sī has the ignoble honor of being the one written into the histories who advised his emperor about a way to get rid of these troublesome, meddling philosophers and all their heated opposing opinions wafting about the palace in Xiányáng, the modern-day city of Xian.

16:37 Lǐ Sī believed a lot less resistance would be felt at the top if there was only… you know… one single political philosophy to rule them all, so to speak. A hundred schools, as far as Lǐ Sī was concerned, was ninety-nine too many. He sold this idea to Qín Shǐhuáng, and in 213 BCE, truly a year that will live in infamy forevermore, a

THE HISTORY OF CHINESE PHILOSOPHY
PART 8

torch was put to all the books that concerned themselves with philosophy, ideology and literature. Technical books, the Yì Jīng and anything that had a Legalist bent, were the only texts allowed.

17:19 Now when I say all these other works were destroyed, let me say not everything got put to the torch. But a lot did, and just as with the fire that gutted the Library of Alexandria, we can only wonder how much knowledge and wisdom was lost to the ages as a result of Qín Shǐhuáng's 213 BCE edict. Any works that could be saved were buried underground until the times changed. It was a huge blow to intellectual discourse and to the cause of preserving China's heritage.

17:54 Three years later, 210 BCE, the Confucianists were silenced when 460 of them were supposedly buried alive. In these two acts, burning the books and burying the scholars, the ultimate goal of having one single state ideology across the land was achieved. And for his hand in all this, Lǐ Sī is going to run the ancient Chinese gauntlet of vilification. Sīmǎ Qiān is not going to be kind to him, and neither will the other Hàn Dynasty historians.

18:30 No one can say if this is truth or fiction, burning the books, burying the scholars. It's been part of Chinese history lore since Sīmǎ Qiān published the first edition of the Shǐ Jì.

18:42 Before we move on, let us not forget that it was Lǐ Sī more than anyone else who managed the projects that

THE HISTORY OF CHINESE PHILOSOPHY
PART 8

were all credited to Qín Shǐhuáng: in Chinese culture, standardizing the characters, weights, measures, currency, and setting in place all the gears, wheels, switches and pulleys of the Chinese State... the complete mechanism.

19:06 Legalism was not for the squeamish. Depending on where you were on the totem pole, life was most unforgiving and harsh. The Hàn swept away the Qín in 206 BCE and carried out a major realignment. But after enjoying a nice time of the stage, Legalism is going to be swept away and dissed entirely.

19:29 And remember Xúnzǐ? He's going to fall from grace real hard for being the teacher of Lǐ Sī and Hán Fēizǐ. Xúnzǐ agreed with the Legalists that people weren't born innately good, but other than that, he was all straight Confucianism with a few nice improvements added on.

19:48 As Liú Bāng began to get his new Hàn dynasty in order, he had to take stock of the situation. He was the first of only two people in Chinese history to have come from a common, non-aristocratic background and lead the fight to found a Dynasty. Zhū Yuánzhāng of the Míng being the other. And Liú Bāng, also known by his temple name Hàn Gāozǔ, he needed some serious legitimizing. Having a guy like him as the emperor, well, something was needed to give him and his new dynasty some shine, not to mention legitimacy.

20:28 It wasn't enough that the Qín Dynasty was finished. A lot of people came out with their swords to give it to

THE HISTORY OF CHINESE PHILOSOPHY
PART 8

them. I'm not comparing it to the Cultural Revolution, but it was a long decade of unpleasantness and when it was over, everyone muttered goodbye and good riddance under their breath.

20:49 And for Confucianism, being the antithesis of Legalism, it was never looking better. And during the Han Dynasty, Confucianism is going to have one heck of a golden age.

21:01 In deconstructing the Qín Dynasty, Hàn Gāozǔ started loosening up the laws. What we would call a capital offense, those were still subject to severe penalties. But for a lot of other things that impacted everyone, things loosened up and life began to settle down, and then once everything was nice and stable. Confucianism began its comeback.

21:25 Hàn Gāozǔ fought for and won everything that had been created and put in place by the Qín. Say what you will about Qín Shǐhuáng... tyrant, a profligate... he put a government structure in place that really allowed the Hàn Dynasty to get off to a flaming hot start. The Hàn will expand the map of China to its greatest extent in BCE times. That was quite a sizable operation to manage and the perfect solution ended up being the Confucianists. They were educated, capable, knew all the ceremonies and rituals, how to read the calendar. They were one-stop shopping for Hàn Gāozǔ.

22:08 So before we continue on and look at the triumph of Confucianism in the Han, let's slip the bookmark in and hold off till next time when we look at the very

 THE HISTORY OF CHINESE PHILOSOPHY
PART 8

consequential but underrated official, Dǒng Zhòngshū and see how he facilitated the embrace of Confucianism by the emperor and the imperial government. This was an embrace that lasted on and off for over two thousand years.

22:33 That's all for next time. This is Laszlo Montgomery thanking you once again for listening. Be sure to come back next time for another exciting episode of the China History Podcast.

 # The History of Chinese Philosophy Part 9

THE TRANSCRIPTS

SUMMARY

Dong Zhongshu and the triumph of Confucianism during the Han Dyansty, Sima Tan and the Six Schools, The first explainers of Confucianism: Liu Xin, Wang Chong, Yang Xiong

TRANSCRIPT

00:00	Welcome back everyone, Laszlo Montgomery here with you again.
00:05	Up to now, we've looked at Confucian philosophy and Legalism. Remember, when you look up Confucianism in the Chinese dictionary, it's simply known as Rú or Rújiā. From these Hundred Schools of thought going back to the Spring and Autumn Period of the Eastern Zhou Dynasty, it was ultimately Confucianism, commencing in the Hàn Dynasty, that triumphed over all the other schools of thought.
00:32	Let's begin by taking a look at how Confucianism made the comeback of the century during the reign of Emperor Hàn Gāozǔ.

THE HISTORY OF CHINESE PHILOSOPHY
PART 9

00:40 After defeating Xiàng Yǔ and after his new Han Dynasty was established, Hàn Gāozǔ had the Confucian officials draw up a whole master plan detailing how they would manage all palace rituals and ceremonies and how to staff the imperial court staffed and how to manage everything that Qín Shǐhuáng left behind. Everything that an imperial court might require down to the imperial regalia and trappings of being an emperor. All of this had to be decided upon and instituted.

01:13 And once all of this was in place, the rough warrior Liú Bāng made the transition to regal emperor Hàn Gāozǔ of China.

01:22 Confucianism began to thrive once again and before long it was safe for everyone to come out. Of the Hundred Schools of Thought that thrived during the Eastern Zhou, many of them didn't make it to the Hàn. Some got snuffed out during the Qín. There was also some consolidation where rival schools of thought joined together. It wasn't what it used to be, but it was a totally new time... When Hàn Gāozǔ sat on the throne in 206 BCE, Confucius had been dead for two hundred seventy-three years. A lot had changed and people knew a lot more now than they used to.

02:00 Confucianism's great moment arrived with the Han Emperor Wǔ, Hàn Wǔdì, 156 to 87 BCE. He was one of China's greatest emperors, he makes it to most top ten of every list. Our focus is not so much on Emperor Wǔ as it is the man behind the man. This was another one of the early greats of Chinese culture and history, Dǒng

THE HISTORY OF CHINESE PHILOSOPHY
PART 9

Zhòngshū 董仲舒.

02:29　He's one of those names like Shēn Bùhài, in that he's also not an A-Lister in Chinese history but he should be. The triumph of Confucianism was mainly due to this person: Dǒng Zhòngshū. And again, it wasn't enough that Confucianism triumphed. Legalism was formally made a scapegoat for all the ills suffered under the Qín. Shāng Yāng, Hán Fēi, Lǐ Sī... they all took a drubbing.

02:57　And the idea of the Mandate of Heaven was first mentioned by Dǒng Zhòngshū, this theory regarding the interaction between heaven and man. The man, being the ruler. Allowing the Mandate of Heaven to slip through his fingers was the easiest and most obvious cause for the Qín's fall and the Hàn's rise.

03:20　The Heavenly Mandate, as introduced by Dǒng, was also like a check on the power of the emperor by the bureaucracy. By establishing the idea of this Mandate of Heaven... this Tiān Mìng... it ran both ways. It gave the emperor and ruling house their most important legitimacy but it also hung over their heads like a sword of Damocles, ready to fall if their fortunes went south or bad emperors, famines, natural disasters or invasion started to signal Heaven's disfavor.

03:54　Let me quote from one of Dǒng's works how he put it: "Heaven establishes kings not on behalf of rulers but on behalf of the people; Therefore if his virtue is sufficient to bring security and happiness to the people, Heaven bestows the Mandate on him; if his evil is sufficient

THE HISTORY OF CHINESE PHILOSOPHY
PART 9

	to injure and harm the people, Heaven withdraws the Mandate."
04:18	Under Han Wǔdì, and with Dǒng Zhòngshū's stewardship, an Imperial University was established in 124 BCE which focused on Confucian teachings. And from this university emerged all these Han era Confucianist scholars who went on to populate the entirety of the Imperial bureaucracy, administration, courts.... everywhere. Confucianism reigned.
04:45	All these officials who came from this university had to pass what we know as the Civil Service Exams. This was also a creation of Dǒng Zhòngshū. These exams institutionalized the meritocracy already put in place during the Qín by the Legalists... and these Zhōu era Confucian classics became the required texts.
05:07	These texts were, during Dǒng Zhòngshū's period of service to the emperor, for the first time, grouped together and classified as the Wǔ Jīng, the Five Classics, which were The Book of Odes, Book of Documents, Book of Rites, the Yì Jīng and the Spring & Autumn Annals. These were the five books you had to master if you had any hope of joining the ranks of the civil service.
05:34	So we can see how Confucianism attained its preeminence during the reign of Hàn Wǔdī and with the help of his chief minister Dǒng Zhòngshū. And the magical year was 136 BCE. That's when Confucianism, by proclamation, became the state ideology.

THE HISTORY OF CHINESE PHILOSOPHY
PART 9

05:55 Confucianism had come under attack almost as soon as Master Kǒng passed away in 479 BCE. The Mohists and others including the Legalists, had pounded hard on Confucianism. Yeah, this Rú School took its lumps. But now it had prevailed over its rival philosophies thanks to its great champion, Dong Zhongshu.

06:19 Sacrifices were decreed in Confucius's honor, his texts were engraved in stone. Confucianism would henceforth always remain the philosophy of the aristocracy. But unlike before the Han Dynasty, the aristocracy was not limited to the nobility. To make it nowadays, all you needed was real talent and virtue. If you were smart and talented enough to climb the ladder, you too could become one of the beautiful people.

06:47 Part of the Han Emperor's conquests involved the 111 BCE defeat of the Nányuè Kingdom down in the southernmost region of China, Guǎngdōng-Guǎngxī. Further south of them was a place called "Yuè Nán" or south of Yuè, which we call Vietnam today. The Chinese went into Vietnam and from that point on starting in the Hàn, with a break here and there through the centuries, there were four periods when China dominated or at the very least heavily influenced Vietnam court politics.

07:22 That's why Confucianism caught on in Vietnam like no other place in Southeast Asia. Same with Daoism and Mahayana Buddhism. Same can be said of Chinese writing as well. The current Vietnamese writing system only became widespread maybe a century ago.

THE HISTORY OF CHINESE PHILOSOPHY PART 9

07:40 I won't get into this right now, but starting right about here, the rivalry between the Confucianists in government and those of the Daoist persuasion began to heat up a notch here. By Hàn Wǔdì's time, it had been about four hundred years since Lǎozǐ's time and a century and a half since Zhuāngzǐ. So you could say Daoism by now was somewhat mature and had spread far and wide, including into the halls of power. Pretty soon the Buddhists will also throw their hat in the ring.

08:14 Dǒng Zhòngshū is also credited with the idea of correlative Confucianism. Here's where philosophy takes on a new twist. Dǒng Zhòngshū came up with a theory that combined Yīn and Yáng and the Five Elements... the Wǔ Xíng... with Confucian thought. He was looking to shine a spotlight on the correlation between human behavior and heaven's will, the interrelatedness of the cosmos and human nature.

08:45 Tiān, heaven, and human beings were both comprised of the forces of Yīn and Yáng, which therefore means there was an intrinsic connection between Heaven and people through the movement and interaction of these forces. Dǒng believed that heaven... Tiān... was both a natural phenomenon and a god of sorts that expressed human will, always trying to warn or reward humankind with all the signs of Heaven's pleasure or displeasure.

09:20 Dǒng Zhòngshū wrote that the universe was broken down into ten parts: Heaven, earth, Yīn, Yáng, the five elements of Wood, Fire Soil, Metal, and Water and humankind. And because people were one of the ten,

THE HISTORY OF CHINESE PHILOSOPHY
PART 9

Dǒng Zhòngshū said cosmology and Confucianism both had an influence on the human and natural worlds. Everything was interrelated, tied together by the forces of Yīn and Yáng.

09:51 The universe, taught Dǒng Zhòngshū, was filled with these ethers of Yīn and Yáng and humans were immersed in these ethers. Change was happening constantly and everyone was affected by everything.

10:06 Yeah, the Confucianism of the Han was not the same as how they practiced it in the late Zhou. As we'll see it was an evolving ideology.

10:15 After the shakeup that happened in the world of Chinese philosophy during the Qin, it ultimately fell on the shoulders of Sīmǎ Tán, father of Sīmǎ Qiān, to sort out the surviving schools of philosophy, to divide them all up and introduce the main ideas each one espoused. This is where we get that neat and tidy bundle of the Six Schools of Philosophy. According to Sīmǎ Tán they were the Yīn Yáng School, the School of Names, the Rú School, the Mohists, Legalism and what he called the Dàodé School but was actually the Daoist school. No one up to Sīmǎ Tán's time was calling anyone a Daoist yet. But now that these myriad of different schools had all been sorted out, Daoism or Dàojiā finally had a specific classification.

11:13 This list would later on be further enhanced by the great Confucian scholar Liú Xīn (劉歆). He lived 46 BCE to 23 CE, the time of Augustus in Rome and Jesus in the Holy

THE HISTORY OF CHINESE PHILOSOPHY
PART 9

Land. This period was also the final years of the Western Han.

11:31 Liú Xīn is remembered for a few things. Firstly he was Curator of the Imperial Library and oversaw an entire makeover of the library, organizing all the surviving Chinese Classics and Commentaries. Liú Xīn took the Hundred Schools and further divided them into ten schools. These were the same six as mentioned by Sīmǎ Tán plus the Schools of Diplomats, Eclectics, Agrarians and Storytellers who were noted as the least important of the ten.

12:04 Liú Xīn explained that these schools all had their origins in different classes of society. He said that the Rú School came from the Ministry of Education... these were the Confucianists mostly. They were all proficient in the Liù Yì (六藝)... the Six Arts... Rites, Music, Archery, Charioteering, Calligraphy and Mathematics. These are among the subjects that a typical Confucian scholar would be proficient in. Liú Xīn said they also stood for human-heartedness and held the ancients in the highest possible esteem.

12:40 The Daoists came from the official historians. The Yin Yang School came from among the astronomers. The Legalists, no surprise, came from the ministry of justice. The School of Names came from the ministry of ceremonies. The Mohists were the temple guardians. The Diplomats School came from the ministry of embassies. The Eclectic School from the councilors who dabbled in multiple ideologies. And the Agrarian School came from

THE HISTORY OF CHINESE PHILOSOPHY PART 9

the ministry of soil and grains and the Story Tellers came from the petty offices and concerned itself mostly with the word on the street.

13:17 So the Han Dynasty really took an inventory of all their philosophy, cosmology, and different schools of thought and got everything all organized and categorized for the first time. Two people emerged during the Han who I wanted to mention. They showed how Confucianism was constantly evolving as people became smarter. And new theories were espoused regarding human beings and the forces of Heaven and nature. That "Confucian APP", you know... it needed an update every so often as new ideas gained followers and acceptance.

13:55 Let's look at Wáng Chōng (王充). He's a nice example of some of the many new ideas and discoveries that had been packed on to all the philosophic thought inherited from the Zhou. By the Hàn, there were a lot of philosophers who went far beyond the thought that came from Confucius, Mèngzǐ and Xúnzǐ too. All kinds of cool stuff was being discovered, and argued, and refuted.

14:20 During this exciting time, there was a split that occurred within the Confucianist doctrine. Two schools emerged. The Old Text School was headed up by Yáng Xióng and Wáng Chōng. They held most sacred those books that had come from the Zhou that had managed to survive the book burning drama of the Qin in 213 BCE. These texts were written in the old style.

THE HISTORY OF CHINESE PHILOSOPHY
PART 9

14:47 The New Text School, on the other hand, used versions of the classics that were more modern and in the style of the Western Hàn.

14:55 Yáng Xióng... not an influential figure but he is remembered for his belief that human nature is neither originally good like Mèngzǐ says nor as bad as what Xúnzǐ said. Yáng Xióng argued that a person's nature came about as a mixture of both.

15:13 Wáng Chōng's work is contained in a source known as the Lùnhéng (論衡) or Balanced Discussions. If there's a word that defined Wáng Chōng, I supposed you can say it was skepticism. Maybe rationalism too. He let it all hang out in the Lùnhéng, spewing forth his doubts in every direction, even questioning Confucius himself and rejecting Hán Fēizǐ altogether. He insisted that those who came before them shouldn't be accepted outright without asking some difficult questions.

15:46 For example, he attacked the Yīn Yáng School's doctrine that a nexus existed between Heaven and man. Wáng Chōng had written that people's place in the universe is like that of a flea or a louse under a jacket or robe. If people acted improperly or properly, morally or immorally—it didn't do anything to change the world. A flea cannot effect changes and neither can man. That was the main thing Wáng Chōng taught in his thought. We can't change Heaven and Heaven sure as heck isn't going to go out of its way to change us. He was not a believer in divine will.

THE HISTORY OF CHINESE PHILOSOPHY PART 9

16:25 | He particularly focused some of his rage against the belief in ghosts. You can have spirits, but he drew the line at those who passed away and came back as ghosts. The rationalist in Wáng Chōng said if this was the case, more people had died in history than were living in his day, so that reasoning right away gave the idea of the dead returning as spirits and ghosts a bad smell in Wáng Chōng's opinion.

16:51 | Wáng Chōng was one of those polymath types who knew a lot about everything. In fact the great 20th century scholar of the history of Chinese science Joseph Needham, he spoke at length about Wáng Chōng's contributions to astronomy, irrigation and meteorology in particular. Like a lot of people who are extremely brilliant and have high IQ's, Wáng Chōng found it hard to get along with those officials he rubbed elbows with.

17:19 | He had this outrage about what Chinese philosophy had degraded to in his time. Confucianism had been made the state ideology by Hàn Wǔdì for over a hundred years already. Confucius was worshipped as a god.

17:33 | The way Wáng Chōng saw Daoism... it had mostly degraded into a religion filled with superstition, lucky talismans and too many people making money as a fēng shuǐ Masters.

17:46 | Wáng Chōng really turned his nose up at this. But despite all the resistance, Daoism was having a real growth spurt during the Hàn. Emperor Huán (漢桓帝) who reigned 146 to 168, even had a temple built at Lǎozǐ's birthplace

THE HISTORY OF CHINESE PHILOSOPHY
PART 9

	where people could go and venerate him.
18:04	Wáng Chōng was going around saying that all those old books and commentaries about the sages needed to be reevaluated and should never be accepted at face value. For example he pointed at something as common as the rain. Wáng Chōng said that the Confucianists will have you believe the rain came from the heavens, but if you study the rain closely, it rains down from a position just above the earth, not from heaven.
18:32	He had a lot to say about Qì. We are going to explore the concept of Qì in detail in a future episode. But Qì is defined as gas, air, breath, smell, weather, and vital energy. It has a lot of meanings, but the one we care most about is the Qì that any living thing possesses, their vital life force. And Qì interacts with the Five Elements and with Yīn and Yáng and that alone, ladies and gentlemans, brings you everything there is in the world as we know it.
19:07	As I said, we've all heard about Qì. That's the same word Qì as in Qìgōng. You've heard of that perhaps? It's already part and parcel of Chinese philosophy in the Hàn. But Qì, the Five Elements, Yin and Yang... they all play an even greater role in Chinese philosophy as we move along the historical timeline.
19:28	Okay, let's put our things away and close up shop. For these past nine episodes we've mostly looked at the History of pre-Confucian and Confucian Philosophy as well as Legalism. We looked at Confucius and those

THE HISTORY OF CHINESE PHILOSOPHY PART 9

who followed him. He wasn't everyone's cup of tea, and as you'll soon see when we explore Daoism, he's downright vilified in some ways.

19:51 | Until then, this is Laszlo Montgomery signing off from Los Angeles California, thanking each and every one of you for listening and for supporting me. I look forward to seeing you once again next time for another exciting episode of the China History Podcast

 The History of Chinese Philosophy Part 10

THE TRANSCRIPTS

SUMMARY

The end of the Han Dynasty, the rise of Buddhism and the rivalries between the three religions, The seeds of Neo-Confucianism are planted, Han Yu, Li Ao, Liu Zongyuan and the Daotong Lineage

TRANSCRIPT

00:00 | Hi everyone, Laszlo Montgomery here. You're listening to the China History Podcast. We're back with more Chinese Philosophy.

00:09 | Before we dive right in, let's take a quick moment to review the main bullet points. We've sort of been jumping all over the place for the sake of trying not to mix things up too badly. But now that we've mixed things up sufficiently enough, it's time to sort it all out and move forward.

00:25 | We're exiting the Han Dynasty, 3rd century CE, and both Confucianism and Daoism have both matured. People in the 3rd century CE are they ever more sophisticated and wise to the ways of the world compared to their ancestors in the previous dynasty.

THE HISTORY OF CHINESE PHILOSOPHY
PART 10

00:44 | By the time of the 200's, Rome had already peaked, the Silk Road by now was close to four hundred years old and after all these centuries of crisscrossing back and forth between east and west and north and south, plenty of new ideas, science, culture and what not, had been spread far and wide and had been picked over and studied in all the main centers of learning along the *Seidenstrasse*.

01:13 | So to your average scholar in the mid 3rd century CE... those philosophers from the Eastern Zhou... that was a completely different age. And the Zhou era understanding of the way of the world compared to such modern times as the 3rd century seemed like the Dark Ages. Philosophy was a way more sophisticated product now with all kinds of standard and upgraded options not available in Mèngzǐ's time.

01:42 | The history of Chinese philosophy timeline usually started with the fall of the Shāng and the establishment of the Zhou. We saw how sage kings from Yáo to the early Western Zhou kings all primed the pump for Chinese civilization. But society had degraded and in this Axial Age, as Karl Jaspers put it... humankind started to ponder in a serious, scientific and organized manner, the great questions of the day and how to make their world a better place.

02:18 | And because there were so many different schools of thought who had their own take on how to handle these great questions, they came to be known as the Hundred Schools... the Zhūzǐ Bǎijiā.

THE HISTORY OF CHINESE PHILOSOPHY
PART 10

02:28 I introduced a few... Dèng Xī, Yáng Zhū, Hán Fēi, Lǐ Sī, Wáng Chōng, Guō Xiàng, Wáng Bì, Xiàng Xiù... And we looked at the major figures of the Rú School starting with its most famous star Kǒngzǐ, Confucius. There were his seventy-seven disciples, Mèngzǐ, Xúnzǐ and many more...

02:51 But by the end of the Han, there were a lot of balls to juggle in the world of Chinese cosmology, epistemology, metaphysics, ethics, politics. Qì, Yīn and Yáng, the Yìjīng, the Celestial Stems, Earthly Branches... everybody was talking to everybody. And as far as Confucianism was concerned, it wasn't like it was in the time of the Great Sage. From here on out, every few generations or so for the remainder of Chinese imperial history, like the APPs on your phone, Confucianism needed constant upgrading.

03:28 We also discussed earlier about Qín Shǐhuáng's chief minister Lǐ Sī, and how he was able to put the kibosh on all philosophic discussion that deviated from the Party Line which in the Qin Dynasty was Legalism. We'll never know what great unknown works were lost to the flames of 213 BCE. Everyone had to keep their head down for a while, but once the Qin self-destructed and the Han Dynasty set itself up in Cháng'ān, philosophy came back with a vengeance... and I hope you didn't mind that for a few events, names and terms, we sort of glossed over... they're going to come up again. So I'm hoping with all the jumping around I had to do, some of these blank spaces can be filled out a little. Keep that Infographic close by.

THE HISTORY OF CHINESE PHILOSOPHY
PART 10

04:19 So let's get to the conclusion of the Han Dynasty. As I mentioned at the end of last episode, once the Han comes crashing down China will remain mostly disunited all the way clear through to the Suí in 589. Yeah, the Western Jìn pulled everything together for a brief while but for the most part, it was a rough three and a half centuries for China.

04:42 But not for Buddhism. Oh baby, this was their time. Buddhism had already made landfall in China during the Han Dynasty, during the time of Hàn Míng Dì, son of Líu Xiù, the Guāngwǔ emperor. And the Buddhist faith spread like an LA wildfire during this chaotic disunited period after the fall of the Han. This was the time of the Six Dynasties or Liù Cháo period that covered from the end of the Three Kingdoms in 280 to the start of the Suí in 589.

05:19 Just as the war and chaos of the Eastern Zhou did for stoking the fires that gave rise to the Hundred Schools, so were the trying times of the Six Dynasties for Buddhism. There's nothing like hardship, hopelessness and suffering to drive the masses of people in droves into the hopeful and calming arms of the Buddha. And not just the peasant folks... the swells too.

05:45 So Buddhism got real energized in China during this post-Han Six Dynasties period and then went into afterburner during the Suí with the patronage of Yáng Jiān, the dynasty founder and his very devout empress.

THE HISTORY OF CHINESE PHILOSOPHY
PART 10

06:01 Nothing like political patronage at the highest possible level to help your cause, no matter spiritual or temporal. And it's in the Sui Dynasty... only two emperors long... the Buddhists in Cháng'ān, the capital, got to test their wings and get a first taste of power close to the royal center. As I said, the Confucians, Daoists and Buddhists would spend the next couple thousand years always trying to muscle in on each other's turf inside these halls of power. This was serious stuff.

06:37 It was during the Sui that Buddhism began to yield Chinese home-grown sects... the Tiantai most notably... that took the basic religion and philosophy from India and Nepal, foreign lands, and remolded it into something that fit Chinese sensibilities and spiritual needs more comfortably and naturally.

07:01 And after 1040 in the Northern Sòng, after moveable type printing takes off... China will become flooded with Buddhist texts. The oldest known printed book is the Diamond Sutra from 868, during the Tang.

07:16 Following the Sui, in the Tang, Daoism enjoyed a nice golden age. There was a long period when Empress Wǔ Zétiān ruled, from 690-705. And she was the best thing that had ever happened to Buddhism up until her time. Empress Wǔ was one of Buddhism's greatest royal patrons, and throughout Chinese imperial history there were many. Under her royal patronage Chán Buddhism, another Chinese flavored version of the religion, rose to great prominence.

THE HISTORY OF CHINESE PHILOSOPHY
PART 10

07:49   It was a pretty logical and easy stretch to put Buddhism and Daoism side by side and find enough commonalities. In fact, in order to draw in new converts, Buddhist monks often would infuse their teachings with little bits and pieces of Daoism so that the newly faithful could get it... so that they could better grasp what Buddhism was all about.

08:14   With Buddhism's meteoric rise and Daoist beliefs becoming second nature to the people, Confucianism found itself under the gun as far as trying to keep up with the competition. The mass popularity of the Tiantai sect... and now Chán Buddhism were really giving Daoism a run for its money.

08:30   Many of the new spiritual and metaphysical ideas presented by these religions had never been considered during Confucius's time. So to keep up with the Joneses and these new beliefs that had been embraced by the populace, Confucianism needed to up its game and maintain relevancy in such modern times.

08:51   What do do in such a case? This was a much discussed issue amongst the Confucian thinkers of the Tang Dynasty... 618-907... By then more than a thousand years had passed since the age of Confucius, Mèngzǐ and Xúnzǐ. Leading Confucians took a look around at the popularity of this Daoist and Buddhist philosophy and had to ask themselves, "What would Kongzi do? What would Mengzi think?" These philosophers during the early Tang had to become those sages of antiquity and channel their ancient thought into the modern context,

THE HISTORY OF CHINESE PHILOSOPHY
PART 10

which was quite complex to say the least.

09:31 Just as Christianity had St. Thomas Aquinas who reconciled Christian thought with the intellectual environment of his day in the 13th century, Tang Confucianists sought to write their own "Summa Theologica" of Confucianism.

09:48 Let's spend some time in the Tang and Song dynasties and see how Chinese Confucian thought spread its wings even wider and then glided into our present age.

09:58 Now you'd think trying to compete with the mass popularity of Daoism and Buddhism was a lost cause, but the Confucianists refused to fold. They might not have had it so good like they did back when Emperor Wu of Han was around, but they still dominated the elite life of aristocrats and in the government bureaucracy.

10:18 During the Tang Dynasty they were fortunate to have as their champion, the great dynasty co-founder Tàizōng. Tang Tàizōng ordered a Confucian Temple be built, and then in 630 he called for all of the Confucian classics to be prepared in new official editions. And from the standardization of these Confucian classics came a flood of new commentaries that picked every aspect of these works apart and analyzed them in a thousand new and different ways.

10:51 And it was these official editions called for by the Táng Tàizōng Emperor as well as the multitude of commentaries that followed in its wake, that formed the

THE HISTORY OF CHINESE PHILOSOPHY
PART 10

	core curriculum studied by all aspiring officials to the imperial government.
11:05	The Tang Dynasty was a great period for all kinds reasons... in the arts, sciences, literature, poetry, in the propagation of tea culture... and of course in Confucian philosophy. There were three noted scholars who I wanted to mention who paved the way for what later on would be called Neo-Confucianism.
11:28	All three of these earliest Tang Confucian reformers lived about the same time... late 8th, early 9th century. This was the time of the Tang emperors from Dàizōng to Wénzōng. These were Hán Yù, Lǐ Áo and Liǔ Zōngyuán. All three scholars combined to revive Confucianism in the wake of Buddhism's relentless growth in popularity, especially during Wǔ Zétiān's time in power during the late 7th century.
11:58	And they will do such a good job that shortly after their passing in the 840's, the very heavily Daoist influenced Tang Emperor Wǔzōng will green-light a government sanctioned persecution of Buddhism in China. Although not a bloody event as persecutions of religions go, many Buddhist schools of thought failed to revive.
12:21	And it wasn't just the Buddhists who felt Emperor Wǔzōng's imperial backlash... other religions deemed "foreign" had to run for cover and lay low until the political winds changed. This, and the Ān Lùshān Rebellion that lasted 755-763, had quite an impact on the ongoing development of Chinese philosophy.

THE HISTORY OF CHINESE PHILOSOPHY
PART 10

12:44 Hán Yù is credited with being the one who launched the revival of Confucianism following this cataclysmic Ān Lùshān Rebellion. In the West, this revived version of Rú philosophy was called Neo-Confucianism. They never called it that in China. They had other terms for this thought. The term Neo Confucianism came from...who else...the Jesuits. French missionary Jean-Joseph-Marie Amiot coined the term in a work published in 1777.

13:19 Hán Yù popularized an idea that caught on quite well. He said The Dào was given to Yáo who passed it on to Shùn who passed it on to Yǔ who passed it on to King Wén to King Wǔ and then to Zhōu Gōng... the Duke of Zhou.

13:35 And it was Zhou Gong, said Hán Yù, who passed this wisdom on to Confucius. And this was how Hán Yù explained it... In the late Tang Dynasty how the Dào and Confucian philosophy crossed paths so to speak. The Dào came all the way from the ancients directly to the Great Sage.

13:56 This lineage of the Confucian tradition, or Dàotǒng, from Yáo, Shùn, Yǔ, King Wén, King Wǔ, Duke of Zhōu, Confucius and then on to Mèngzǐ, is one of Hán Yù's great achievements. Hán Yù claimed, however, that after Mengzi, this lineage ended. We'll see in a bit how one of the five founders of Neo-Confucianism, Chéng Hào, was named as the heir to Mengzi in carrying on this Dàotǒng lineage.

THE HISTORY OF CHINESE PHILOSOPHY
PART 10

14:26 Hán Yù is considered to be the most important of the Tang Confucian scholars. He was another one of China's great writers and polymaths as well as an important political figure of his time. All his writings, his essays, are all highly ranked and admired, and the Tang Dynasty really cranked out a lot of amazing talent.

14:48 A part of his literary efforts were directed at draining the swamp in the capital at Luòyáng of Buddhist influence. One of his more famous works is called the Memorial on Bone Relics of the Buddha, the famous Jiànyíng Fógǔ Biǎo 堅硬佛骨表, where, in 819, he really tore into what he described as all this ridiculous Buddhist black magic and the travesty of these holy relics popping up everywhere.

15:15 Hán Yù was a little too critical of the Emperor Xiànzōng, chastising him in this work for going along with all these Buddhist activities and ceremonies, hoodwinking an essentially ignorant and superstitious populace. Hán Yù said these Buddhists hurt more than they helped, and of course, their faith and ideology were a foreign import and not a domestic product. For daring to speak out the way he did, Xiànzōng called for Hán Yù ‹s execution. But Hán Yù came from a top drawer family and was very respected and renowned and had friends in high places who got him off the hook.

15:55 Hán Yù instead got demoted and banished to Cháozhōu, Guangdong province. So you know he ate well and was never in short supply of fine culture, and seafood. He laid low in Cháozhōu until Xiànzōng died in 820. Under

THE HISTORY OF CHINESE PHILOSOPHY
PART 10

	the next emperor, Mùzōng, he was brought back to the capital but only lived for a few more years. He was the great champion to the Confucianists, bringing back all these values that everyone believed had been corrupted or lost.
16:25	And Han Yu wasn't terribly fond of the Daoists either, but he let them partially off the hook, saying at least they were a Chinese home-grown philosophy, as misguided as it was.
16:38	Hán Yù, with single-minded purpose dedicated his life, and even risked his life, for the restoration of Confucianism to its rightful place as the one state ideology, just like the old days of Hàn Wǔdì. In the Táng Dynasty Hán Yù promoted the traditional Confucian idea of the sage as the proper role model for human self-cultivation.
17:04	And more well-known, perhaps, is that it was Hán Yù and his colleagues who reached onto the shelf of all the Chinese Classics and commentaries and picked from amongst them only four texts that they considered the most important of all… The Zhōng Yōng, Dàxué, Lúnyǔ and the Mèngzǐ. The Doctrine of the Mean, the Great Learning, the Analects of Confucius and the Mengzi. And henceforth, and even into our day, we call this collection the Sì Shū… the Four Books.
17:38	Another revolutionary idea espoused by Hán Yù was his claim that it was Mèngzǐ more than anyone else who captured the essence of Confucian thought. And Hán

THE HISTORY OF CHINESE PHILOSOPHY
PART 10

Yù's colleague Lǐ Áo considered himself the true heir to Mèngzǐ. He also believed what Hán Yù had taught about the Transmission of the Dào from Yáo to Confucius as gospel. Lǐ Áo, however, parted ways with his colleague on Buddhism. He didn't reject it as much as Hán Yù did. In fact, Lǐ Áo's thought actually contains some Buddhist influence.

18:16 As far as Hán Yù's impact on Chinese culture, in literature and the written language in particular, he's one of those characters who we reserve the P-word for.... "Profound". He restored Confucianism in the Tang and planted the seeds for Neo-Confucianism that would burst onto the scene during the salad years of the Northern Song Dynasty, and that's what we're going to cover next.

18:40 Before we begin our discussion of the Five Founders of Neo-Confucianism, let me make a few broad stroke remarks about what it is essentially... I'm sure many or even most of you have heard this term before....

18:54 Neo-Confucianism. In a sound byte, I guess you can consider it to be a kind of synthesis of Confucianism, Buddhism and Daoism. Confucian ethics with Daoist and Buddhist metaphysical principles. The Tang Confucian reformers, in order to stay current with the times and the ever-expanding sophistication of humankind, sought to offer a kind of cosmological foundation for Confucian values.

THE HISTORY OF CHINESE PHILOSOPHY
PART 10

19:24	They tried to use cosmology to explain their Confucian world. Cosmology: Yǔzhòuxué, from the Greek: *Kosmos*....World and *Logia*, the study of. The study of the origin of the universe, how it developed and how it all fits together.
19:42	In the Tang, philosophers for the first time began this march to tie together cosmology with the ethics and social principles of Confucianism.
19:53	Neo-Confucianism was a kind of movement to also re-assert Chinese values as well as the superiority of the Confucianism. The Neo-Confucianists of the Sòng called for getting reacquainted with the teachings of the Confucian classics.
20:08	The call also went out to shed essential Confucianist thought of any and all Daoist or Buddhist corruption, and bring back that purposeful humanism, rationalism, and ethics that lie at the core of Confucian philosophy.
20:24	And most importantly, these Neo-Confucianists wanted to make Confucius relevant to these 11th century times. But as far as the separate fundamental ideas of Daoism and Buddhism... some say the Neo-Confucianists followed them even more than the Daoists and Buddhists themselves.
20:43	And before we move on to more Chinese Philosophy, let's lower the curtain for now. Please think about coming back once more.

THE HISTORY OF CHINESE PHILOSOPHY
PART 10

20:51 | And until that time when we meet again, this is Laszlo Montgomery signing off from Santa Monica again… but not for long. Thanks for listening, and I already can't wait to see you again next time for another exciting episode of the China History Podcast.

HISTORY OF CHINESE PHILOSOPHY COMPLETE TERMS LIST

Pinyin/Term	Chinese	English/Meaning
Ān Lùshān Rebellion	安史之乱	Rebellion that began 755 and devastated Tang China, ending in 763
Ānhuì	安徽	Province in China
Ānyáng	安阳	Capital of the Shang Dynasty
Art of War	孙子兵法	Sun Tzu's all time best seller
Bà	霸	A Hegemon, the leader of feudal lords during the Zhou era
Bā Guà	八卦	The Eight Trigrams
Bǎi Jiā	百家	The Hundred Schools
Cài	蔡国	Zhou Era state in central China bordering Chen and Chu
Cài Lún	蔡伦	41-121 CE Han era inventor of paper making.
Chán Buddhism	禅	Known as Zen in Japan, a sect of Buddhism
Cháng'ān	长安	Capital of a few dynasties. Located near present day Xian
Cháozhōu	潮州	One of the great and historic cities of southern Guangdong
Chén	陈国	Zhou Era state in central China north of Cai
Chéng	诚	Sincerity, authenticity
Chéng Hào	程颢	One of the Five Founders of Neo-Confucianism, lived 1032-1085

Chéng Yí	程颐	Brother to Cheng Hao, one of the five founders of Neo Confucianism, lived 1033-1107
Chéng-Zhū School.	程朱理学	Also called Lixue, the school of Cheng Yi and Zhu Xi
Chénghuà	明成化	Emperor of China who lived 1447-1487
Chǔ	楚国	Located around Hubei, Central China. One of the Warring States of the Eastern Zhou
Chūnqiū	春秋	Spring and Autumn Annals chronicles the years of Lu State from 722 to 481 BCE
Dà Xué	大学	The Great Learning (one of the Four Books)
Dà Zhuàn	大专	The Great Commentary from the Ten Wings
Dàizōng	唐代宗	Tang emperor, lived 727-779
Dào	道	The Way or Path, The Tao (Dao), take your choice. Also, The Way that is discussed by the Neo-Confucianists is the Way that controls each separate category of things in the universe
Dàodéjīng	道德经	The Classic of the Tao, also known as The Laozi or Tao Teh Ching
Dàojiā	道家	Daoism, the philosophy
Dàojiào	道教	Daoism, the religion
Dàotǒng	道统	Lineage, or passing of the Dao of the Confucian tradition
Daoxue	道学	The teaching of the way or Lǐxue or the teaching of principle
Dàozàng	道藏	The collected works of Daoism. The Daoist Canon
Dàxué	大学	The Great Learning (one of the Four Books)
Dé	德	Virtue
Dèng Xī	邓析	Pre-Confucian philosopher. Lived 545 to 501 BCE

Dǒng Zhòngshū	董仲舒	Advisor to the Han Emperor Wu 179-104 BCE and a champion of Confucianism
Duì Niú Tán Qín	对牛弹琴	Playing a lute to an ox, wasting your time telling someone about something or to do something
Duke Āi of Lǔ	鲁哀公	Reigned in Lu State 494-468 BCE
Duke of Zhou	周公	Son of King Wen, brother of King Wu
Duke Xiàn of Zhèng	郑献公	Ruled in Zheng State from 513-501 BCE
Duke Xiào of Qín	秦孝公	Lived 381-338 BCE. Employed Shang Yang to institute all kinds of reforms that bore fruit a century later
Emperor Huán	汉桓帝	Eastern Han emperor who reigned 146 to 168 CE
Empress Xiǎochéngjìng	小城敬皇后	The Ming Hongzhi Emperor's one true love
Fāngshì	方士	Daoist practitioners of alchemy, astrology, divination, fēng shuǐ and a whole lot more
Fēng Shuǐ	风水	(in Chinese thought) a system of laws considered to govern spatial arrangement and orientation in relation to the flow of energy (qi), and whose favorable or unfavorable effects are taken into account when siting and designing buildings
Féng Yǒulán	冯友兰	1895-1990 author of the "A Short History of Chinese Philosophy." He was a very distinguished Chinese philosopher who did much to spread its popularity around the world
Fú Xī	伏羲	Mythical Sovereign who lived fro 2953 to 2838 BCE
Fújiàn	福建	Coastal province in China, famous for a whole bunch of reasons

Gāo Kǎo	高考	China's annual "SAT Exam" that determines which university you can get into
Gǎogàn zǐdì	高干子弟	The Princeling Class
Gě Hóng	葛洪	Lived 284-364 during Eastern Jin. China's most famous alchemist from ancient times.
géwù	格物	investigation of things, essentially book learning or learning by observation
gōng	功	Efficiency in needlework
guàcí	卦辞	A judgment, defines the meaning of the hexagram in the Yi Jing
Guǎn Zhòng	管仲	720-645 BCE Great reformer and statesman of the Qi State. Advisor to the ruler Duke Huan. Confucius thought highly of him
Guǎngdōng province	广东省	China's southernmost province, if you don't count Hainan
Guǎngxī	广西	Province in southwest China, just north and west of Guangdong
Guìyáng	贵阳	Capital of Guizhou province
Guìzhōu	贵州	Province in west-central China
Guō Xiàng	郭象	Lived 252-312 CE. Influential Xuanxue thinker. His revision and commentary on the Zhuangzi is a masterwork.
Guōdiàn Village	郭店	Site of a treasure trove of ancient relics, unearthed in 1993. Located near Jingmen, Hubei
Hàn Dynasty	汉朝	China's 2nd imperial dynasty following the Qin. Ran four hundred years from 206 BCE to 220 CE
Hán Fēi	韩非	Also known as Han Feizi. Legalist philosopher who lived 280-233 BCE. Studied under Xunzi. A colleague of Li Si (much to his later regret)

Hàn Gāozǔ	汉高祖	The founding emperor of the Han Dynasty, formerly known as Liu Bang
Hàn Míng Dì	汉明帝	Second emperor of the Eastern Han, lived 28-75 CE
Hán State	韩国	One of the seven Warring States of the Eastern Zhou
Hàn Wǔdì	汉武帝	One of China's greatest emperors. Lived from 156 to 87 BCE. Han Emperor who reigned gloriously from 141-87 BCE
Hán Yù	韩愈	Literary great in China who had few peers. Lived 768-824. Also a great statesman
Hángzhōu	杭州	Zhejiang city, home of Alibaba and the Southern Song Dynasty
Hànlín Yuàn	翰林院	The Hanlin Academy
Hànxúe	汉学	As opposed to the Sòngxué (宋学) of Zhū Xī. The study of the works produced in the Han
Hé Tǔ	河图	The Yellow River Map
Héběi	河北	Another old old province of China
Hēilóngjiāng	黑龙江	One of the three provinces of Manchuria
Hénán province	河南省	One of the most ancient of provinces anywhere on earth. Their Tourism slogan is "Where China Began"
Hóngdòushā	红豆沙	Red Bean Soup...the classic southern Chinese banquet closer classic
Hóngwǔ Emperor	洪武帝	The Ming Dynasty founder and not a fan of Mengzi
Hóngzhì	明弘治	Emperor of China who lived 1470-1505
Huáng-Lǎo	黄老	The Yellow Emperor - Laozi form of Daoism (came later than the Lao-Zhuang form)
Huángdì	黄帝	The Yellow Emperor
Huángjí Jīngshì	皇极经世	Shao Yong's "The Book of Supreme Ordering Principles"

Huángjīn shídài	黄金时代	A Golden Age
Huáxià	华夏	Ancient core China. The collected tribes of the ancient Yellow River Valley civilization
Húběi	湖北	Province located in Central China
Huì Shī	惠施	Verbal sparring partner of Zhuangzi, also called Huìzǐ 惠子
Huīzōng	宋徽宗	Northern Song emperor who brought the house down
Huǒ Shī	火师	a ceremonial post at the royal court that involved anything having to do with fire
Jī	姬	Surname of the Zhou Dynasty founding family, all surnamed Jī
Jī Chāng	姬昌	King Wen's name (surnamed Ji)
Jī clan	姬家族	the founders of the Zhou Dynasty
Jī family	姬家族	The founding family of the Zhou Dynasty
Jì Sūn Shì	季孙氏	Viscount Jì Sūn
Jiā Lǐ	家礼	The Book of Family Rituals set everyone straight on the rituals, ceremonies
Jiājìng	明嘉靖	Emperor of China who lived 1507-1567
Jiāngxī	江西	Province in south central China
Jiànyíng Fógǔ Biǎo	见迎佛骨表	Memorial on Bone Relics of the Buddha CE 819
Jié	夏桀	The venal last king of the Xia Dynasty who may have lived 1728-1625 BCE
Jìn Sī Lù	近思录	Zhu Xi's "Reflections on Things at Hand"
Jīn Yōng	金庸	Pen name of the great and venerable Dr. Louis Cha Leung-yung
Jǐng	周景王	Followed his father King Ling as Zhou monarch. he reigned 544-520 BCE

Jīngmén	荆门	Located in Hubei province west of Wǔhàn. Jimgmen is the sister city of North Glengarry in Eastern Ontario, Canada
Jìnshì degree	进士	The highest degree earned from passing the Civil Service exams
Jiǔ Chí Ròu Lín	酒池肉林	The Wine Pool and Meat Forest
Jìxià Xué Gōng	稷下学宫	The Jixia Academy, established in the State of Qi in 318 BCE by Duke Xuan. A lot of great philosophers got their start there
Jūnzǐ	君子	A man of noble character, of virtue, an ideal man whose character embodied the virtue of benevolence and whose acts were in accordance with the rights and with rightness (Thanks Pleco)
Jūnzǐ	君子	A gentleman, in the Confucian sense
Kaifeng	开封	City in Henan. Former capital of the Northern Song
King Jié of Xià	夏桀	The venal last king of the Xia Dynasty who may have lived 1728-1625 BCE
King Nǎn	周赧王	The Last Zhou Dynasty king, deposed in 256 BCE
King Wén	周文王	1152-1056 BCE, founder of the Zhou Dynasty and a role model for what it means to be a virtuous and benevolent ruler
King Wǔ	周武王	Son of King Wen and no less a standup guy. Also helped to found the Zhou. Older brother to the Duke of Zhou
King Yíng Zhèng	秦嬴政	The King of Qin who later founded a dynasty
King Zhòu Xīn of Shāng	商纣辛	The venal final king of the Shang Dynasty, 1075-1046 BCE
Kǒng Miào	孔庙	The Temple of Confucius

Kǒng Qiū	孔丘	Confucius's name
Kǒngfūzǐ	孔夫子	Confucius
Kǒngzǐ	孔子	Confucius - 551-479 BCE
Kòu Ròu	扣肉	Braised pork belly dish
Kūn	坤	The second hexagram Kūn is six rows of broken lines....pure Yīn
Lǎo Dān	老聃	Perhaps a third name that Laozi might have gone by
Lǎo-Zhuāng	老庄	The most commonly known form of Daoism, named for the two most important texts, The Laozi and The Zhuangzi
lǎobǎixìng	老百姓	The Chinese People (the old hundred surnames)
Laǒzǐ	老子	Also known as Lao Tzu. The Old Master, Died around 531 BCE. The work he is known for, the Daidejing, is also known as The Laozi
Lǎozǐ	老子	Also known as Lao Tzu, considered the founder of Daoism and writer of the Dao De Jing. Died in 531 BCE
Lǐ	理	Inner essence or principle
Lǐ Aó	李傲	Tang era philosopher and literary figure and writer of the 来南录, the first travel diary of its kind.
Lǐ Bái	李白	One of the greatest poets in Chinese history, lived 701-762
Lǐ Dān	李聃	Or it could have been this one that Laozi went by
Lǐ Ěr	李耳	Laozi's alleged real name
Lǐ Jì	礼记	The Book of Rites

Lǐ Sī	李斯	280-208 BCE, Legalist great and minister to the Qin Emperor. He had Han Fei done in!
Liáng Zhī	良知	Innate knowledge
Lièzǐ	列子	Philosopher who lived from 450-375
Liú Bāng	刘邦	One of Fortune's Favorites, the founder of the Han Dynasty, later known as Han Gaozu
Liù Cháo	六朝	The Six Dynasties period that covered from the end of the Three Kingdoms in 280 to the start of the Suí in 589
Liú Jǐn	刘瑾	Infamous Ming Dynasty eunuch. Lived from 1451-1510
Liù Jīng	六经	The Six Classics which became the Five Classics after the Yuè Jīng, the Classic of Music was dropped from the list.
Liú Xīn	刘歆	46 BCE to 23 CE Curator of the Imperial Library
Liù Yì	六艺	The Six Arts...Rites, Music, Archery, Charioteering, Calligraphy and Math
Liǔ Zōngyuán	柳宗元	773-819 - Tang literary great who synthesized bits of Confucianism, Daoism and Buddhism
Liùshísì Guà	六十四卦	The Sixty-four hexagrams
Lǐxué	理学	One of the two main schools of Neo Confucianism, The School of Lǐ, or Principle
Lǔ	鲁国	Neighboring state to Qi in Shandong Province. Qi to the north, Lu to the south. Confucius came from Lu
Lǚ Bùwéi	吕不韦	Early supporter of Ying Zheng (a.k.a. Qin Shihuang)
Lǚ Dìng Gōng	鲁定公	Duke Ding of Lǔ
Lù Jiǔyuān	陆九渊	Song era philosopher, lived 1139 to 1193

Lù Xiàngshān	陆象山	The Master of Xiàngshān, also known as Lu Jiuyuan
Lù-Wáng School	陆王心学	School of the Mind....or Xīnxué....This was the thought of Lù Jiǔyuān and Wáng Shǒurén
Lùnhéng	论衡	Balanced Discussions
Lùnhéng	论衡	Published in 80 CE, contains critical essays written by Wang Chong. Needham called the work "Discourses Weighted in the Balance"
Lúnyǔ	论语	The Analects of Confucius (one of the Four Books)
Luò Shū	洛书	The Luo Shu Square
Luó Zhènyù	罗振玉	One of the first scholars to decipher the ancient oracle bone script
Luòyáng	洛阳	Located in Henan. Capital of a few dynasties
Lǔshì Chūnqiū	吕氏春秋	Mr. Lü's Spring and Autumn Annals, a compendium of the philosophies of the Hundred Schools, compiled around 239 BCE under Lü Buwei's patronage
Mǎwángduī	马王堆	Ancient Han Dynasty tomb discovered intact in 1973
Mèng Kē	孟轲	Mengzi, who lived 372 to 289 BCE
Mèng Mǔ	孟母	母 means mother. Mèng Mǔ means Mengzi's mother
Mèng Mǔ Sān Qiān	孟母三迁	Mengzi's mother moved three times (to find the perfect place to raise her son)
Méngchéng	蒙城	Zhuangzi's birthplace, located in Anhui province, Bozhou Prefecture, Chengguan County

Mèngzǐ	孟子	Confucian philosopher who lived from 372-289 BCE, Latinized name was Mencius
Miáo	苗族	The largest ethnic group in Guizhou, also known as The Hmong in the US
Míng	明朝	Ming Dynasty 1368-1644
Míng Jiā	名家	The School of Names
Mò Dí	墨翟	He said all you need is love. He lived 470 to 391 BCE
Mòzǐ	墨子	Philosopher who lived 470-391 BCE. Confucius's first naysayer
Mùzōng	唐穆宗	Tang emperor, lived 795-824
Nányuè	南越	Kingdom down in the southernmost region of China
nèipiān	内篇	The Inner Chapters of the Dao De Jing
Níngbō	宁波	Coastal city in Zhejiang
Nǚ Wá	女娲	Wife (or maybe sister) or Fuxi
Ōuyáng Xiū	欧阳修	Song era statesman and great man of arts and letters, lived 1007-1072. Featured in CHP episode #71
Pī Lín Pī Kǒng	批林批孔	1973 Criticize Confucius Criticize Lin Biao That lasted three years
Qí State	齐国	Zhou Era state located in Shandong
Qì	气	Breath or your "life force", vital energy, energy of life, substance and matter
Qí Huán Gōng	齐桓公	Duke Huán of the State of Qí
Qí Jǐng Gōng	齐景公	Ruler in Qi from 547-490 BCE
Qí State	齐国	One of the seven Warring States, located in Shandong
Qí Xuān Gōng	齐宣公	Ruler of Qi State from 455-405 BCE
Qián	乾	The first hexagram Qián is six rows of solid lines.....pure yáng.

Qiánlóng Emperor	乾隆帝	One of China's great emperors, ruling 1735-1796
Qìgōng	气功	An ancient Chinese health care system that integrates body postures, breathing techniques and focused intention.
Qín	秦	First a Warring State and later a short-lived but influential dynasty 221 - 206 BCE
Qín Shǐhuáng	秦始皇	The first emperor of China, lived 259-210 BCE, also known as Ying Zheng
Qīng	清朝	The Qing Dynasty 1644-1911
Qūfù	曲阜	Confucius's birthplace and site of the main Confucian temple
Rén	仁	humaneness
Rénběnzhuyì	人本主义	Humanism
Rénzōng	仁宗	The fourth Yuan Dynasty emperor, a friend to Confucianism, lived 1285-1320
róng	容	Physical charm
Rú	儒家	The Chinese term for Confucianism
Sān Cóng Sì Dé	三从四德	The Three Obedience's and the Four Virtues
Sānhuáng Wudì	三皇五帝	The Three Sovereigns and Five Emperors (see CHP episode 60)
Shāndōng	山东	Coastal province in China where Lu and Qi States were located
Shāng	商朝	First dynasty in China for which there is archaeological proof. Ran from roughly 1600 to 1046 BCE
Shāng Dynasty	商朝	First dynasty in China for which there is archaeological proof. Ran from roughly 1600 to 1046 BCE, preceded the Zhou Dynasty
Shāng King Zhòu Xīn	商纣辛	The venal final king of the Shang Dynasty

Shàng Shū	尚书	Book of Documents
Shāng Yāng	商鞅	Left a huge mark on the development and triumph of Legalist thought. Lived 390 to 338 BCE
Shāngqiū	商丘	City in Song State where Confucius's people came from. Located today in eastern Henan
Shāngzǐ / Shāng Jūn Shū	商子/商君书	The work written by Shang Yang
Shǎnxī	陕西	Shanxi's next door neighbor, written as Shaanxi 陕西 to differentiate it from Shanxi 山西
Shānxi	山西	Ancient province in northern China
Shào Yōng	邵雍	One of the five founders of Neo-Confucianism, lived 1011-1077
Shàoxīng	绍兴	City in northern Zhejiang
Shēn Bùhài	申不害	Lived 400-337 BCE. Along with Shen Dao, he was a major influence on Han Fei
Shèn Dào	慎到	Philosopher who lived 350-275 BCE. Had a big impact on later Legalism
Shěn Kuò	沈括	One of the greatest polymaths China ever produced. Lived during the Northern Song from 1031-1095
Shèngrén	圣人	A saint, sage, wise person
Shénzōng	神宗	Song emperor. Lived 1048-1085
Shì	士	The knightly class. They formed the backbone of the Ru School, mainly means scholar or soldier
Shǐ Jì	史记	The Record of the Grand Historian, written by the father-son team of Sima Tan and Sima Qian
Shī Jīng	诗经	The Book of Odes

Shí Yì	十翼	The Ten Wings, ethical commentaries to the hexagrams written by Confucius (or so it's said)
Shísān Jīng	十三经	The 13 Confucian Classics
Shíyì	十翼	The Ten Wings (or Commentaries on the Yi Jing) written by Confucius (or so they say)
Shùn	舜	Legendary Sage King who followed Yao and ruled 2356-2255 BCE
Sì Shū	四书	The Four Books
Sìkù Quánshū	四库全书	The Complete Library in Four Sections One of Qianlong's gifts to posterity, 36,381 volumes, 2.3 million pages, 800 million characters
Sīmǎ Qiān	司马迁	Han era writer of the Record of the Grand Historian. Also called the Herodotus of China
Sīmǎ Tán	司马谈	Father of Sima Qian. He began the Records of the Grand Historian and his son finished it up.
Sòng	宋国	Zhou era state in eastern Hénán and a tad of Western Shandong
Sòng Dynasty	宋朝	One of the great dynasties of China 960-1276
Sòng Xué	宋学	Song Studies, a general term for Neo-Confucianism
Sū Shì / Sū Dōngpō	苏轼 / 苏东坡	Northern Song literary great, featured in CHP episode 175
Suí	隋朝	Short-lived but important dynasty 581-618
Sūnzǐ	孙子	the Art of War....written by Sun Tzu, Master Sūn....
Tài Jí	太极	The Supreme Ultimate represented by the Yin Yang symbol

Tài Jí symbol	太极图	The Yin Yang symbol, the Supreme Ultimate, credited to Zhou Dunyi
Táiběi	台北	Largest city in Taiwan, usually written in English as Taipei
Táiběi Yángmíngshān	台北阳明山	The Yangmingshan district in northern Taipei, named after you know who
Tàijí	太极	The Supreme Ultimate
Tàijí Tǔ	太极图	(The Diagram of the Supreme Ultimate (see above Taiji Symbol)
Tàijí Tǔ Shuō	太极图说	Zhou Dunyi's "Explanation of the Diagram to the Supreme Ultimate"
Tàizōng	太宗	Co-founder and 2nd emperor of the Tang Dynasty
Tàocān	套餐	A set course meal
The Wǔ Cháng: rén, yì, lǐ, zhì, and xìn	五常：仁，义，礼，智，信	The Five Constant Virtues: benevolence, righteousness, propriety, wisdom and fidelity
Three Huan Families of Lǔ (The Sān Huán)	三桓	The three most powerful political forces in Lu State: Mèng Sūn Shì (孟孙氏), Shū Sūn Shì (叔孙氏) and Jì Sūn Shì (see below)
Tiān	天	Heaven
Tiān Dì Rén	天地人	Heaven - Earth - Humans
Tiān Lǐ	天理	Cheng Hao said Heaven and Lǐ were one and the same
Tiān Mìng	天命	The Mandate of Heaven
Tiāntāi	天台	Known as Tendai in Japan, a sect of Buddhism that holds the Lotus Sutra in particular high esteem
Treaty of Nanjing	南京条约	Signed in 1842, the most famous of the Unequal Treaties

wàipiān	外篇	The Outer Chapters
Wáng	王	A surname that means King
Wáng Bì	王弼	Short-lived philosopher (226-249), wrote important commentaries on the Dao De Jing and Yi Jing. He was also a scholar of Xuanxue (see below)
Wáng Chōng	王充	Great Han era philosopher who lived around 27-100
Wáng Huá	王华	Father of Wang Yangming
Wáng Shǒurén	王守仁	Neo-Confucian philosopher who lived 1472 to 1529. Better known perhaps as Wang Yangming
Wáng Yángmíng.	王阳明	Neo-Confucian philosopher who lived 1472 to 1529. Also known as Wang Souren
Wáng Yìróng	王懿荣	Discoverer of the Shang Dynasty Oracle Bones
Wèi (River)	渭河	Major tributary of the Yellow River
Wèi (State)	魏国	One of the northern Warring States
Wénzōng	文宗	Tang emperor, lived 809-840
Western Jìn	西晋	Dynasty that ran 265 to 316 in the West and 317-420 in the east
Western Zhou	西周	Founded by King Wen in 1046 BCE. It ran until 771 BCE
Wong Tai Sin Temple	黄大仙庙	Temple located in Hong Kong located at the Wong Tai Sin MTR stop
Wǔ cháng	五常	The Five Bonds - The five relationships between Ruler to the ruled, father to son, husband to wife, elder brother to younger brother and friend to friend
Wǔ Jīng	五经	The Five Classics

Wǔ Xíng	五行	Five Elements: Fire-Water-Wood-Metal-Soil, the Five Activities, the Five Agents and the Five Dynamic Interacting Forces
Wǔ Zétiān	武则天	Empress Regnant of the Zhou Dynasty, the dynasty she founded in 690. Also Empress Dowager of the Tang Dynasty. Quite a woman of accomplishments!
wújí	无极	The ultimate of non-being
Wúwéi	无为	Non-action, hard to explain
Wǔxiá novels	武侠小说	A genre of Chinese fiction filled with martial artists and brave characters. Jin Yong is the most famous writer of this genre.
Wǔzōng	武宗	Tang emperor who lived 814-846. Carried out a lot of religious persecution
Xià Dynasty	夏朝	A mythical dynasty that preceded the Shang
Xiá Shì	侠士	Knights-errant; practiced swordsman; gallant fighter; swashbuckler
Xīān	西安	Present day capital of Shaanxi Province. Also the site of several ancient capitals during the Zhou, Han and Tang
Xiàng Xiù	向秀	Lived 227-272. His writings on the Zhuangzi inspired Guo Xiang. One of the great scholars of his day
Xiāngkè	相克	The Mutual Conquest Series of the 5 Elements: wood conquers earth, metal conquers wood, fire conquers metal, water conquers fire, and earth conquers water
Xiāngshēng	相生	The Mutual Generation Series of the 5 Elements: wood produces fire, fire produces earth, earth produces metal, metal produces water, and water produces wood.
Xiányáng	咸阳	Near present day Xian, the capital of the Qin State and the Dynasty

Xiànzōng	唐宪宗	Tang emperor who lived 778-820
Xiǎo rén	小人	the Small Person or Lower Person compared with that of the Jūnzǐ
Xīmíng	西铭	Zhang Zai's "Western Inscription"
Xìn	信	integrity, sincerity
Xīn	心	Heart, mind
Xīn xué	心学	The School of the Mind
Xìng Shàn	性善	The theory of Mengzi that people are by nature good
Xuánxúe	玄学	Dark learning - a mystical school developed in the 3rd and 4th centuries, characterized by metaphysical speculations seeking to adapt Daoist theories to a Confucian melieu. Mysterious learning. Also called Neo-Daoism. Can also mean metaphysics among other definitions
Xuánzōng	玄宗	Tang Emperor who lived from 685-762 and reigned from 713-756. The longest reigning of the Tang emperors
Xún Kuàng	荀况	Also known as Xunzi, lived 313 to 238 BCE
Xúnzǐ	荀子	Master Xun, Confucian philosopher who lived from 313-238 BCE
Xūqiú	需求	Demand
yán	言	Propriety in speech
Yáng Jiān	杨坚	Founder of the Sui Dynasty, a.k.a. Sui Wendi
Yáng Xióng	杨雄	Philosopher who lived from 53 BCE to 18 CE
Yáng Zhū	杨朱	Zhou era philosopher 440-360 BCE
Yáng Zhū	杨朱	A philosopher with an interesting take on life 440-360 BCE. He espused seeking pleasure whenever, wherever

Yáng Zhū	杨朱	Philosopher who lived 440-360 who advised toseek pleasure whenever wherever
Yángmíngshān	阳明山	District north of Taipei
Yángmíngshān Sénlín Gōngyuán	阳明山森林公园	The Yangmingshan Forest Park in southern Hunan
yǎngshēng	养生	A sub-category of Dào Jiào (道教)....the Daoist religion.... it means to preserve or enhance your life
Yáo	尧	The legendary Sage King, revered by Confucius who may have lived from 2356-2255 BCE
yáo cí	爻辞	The individual line statements of the Yi Jing, two to thirty characters in length
Yì	义	righteousness
Yì Jīng	易经	The I Ching or Book of Changes
Yílǐ	仪礼	Ceremonies and Rites
Yīn Yáng	阴阳	The two opposing forces that control all change and transformation in the world, and the universe too
Yǐn Xǐ	尹喜	The last one to see or speak with Laozi
Yíng Zhèng	嬴政	Founder of the Qin Dynasty
Yīngzōng	宋英宗	Song emperor. Lived 1032-1067
Yǔ	禹	Yu the Great, founder of the Xia Dynasty, revered for his sacrifices in taming the floods of his day
Yǔ the Great	大禹	(see above) Mythical founder and Sage King of the Xia Dynasty, also called "Great Yu"
Yù Xióng / Yùzǐ	鬻熊 / 鬻子	Master Yu, Pre-Confucian philosopher who served the first Zhou kings
Yuè Lìng	月令	The Monthly Commands
Yuè Nán	越南	Vietnam

Yúnnán	云南	Southwestern province of China
Yúyáo	余姚	City in northern Zhejiang
Yǔzhòuxé	宇宙学	Cosmology
Yùzǐ	鬻子	Pre-Confucian philosopher who served the first Zhou kings
Zhāng Dàolíng	张道陵	Founder of the Way of the Celestial Master sect of Daoism
Zhāng Zài	张载	One of the five founders of Neo Confucianism, lived 1020-1077
Zhànguó shídài	战国时代	The Warring States Period
Zhào	赵	A common Chinese surname. The surname of the family who ruled during the Song Dynasty
Zhào Kuāngyìn	赵匡胤	The founding emperor of the Song Dynasty, also known as Song Taizu
Zhèng	郑国	One of the Eastern Zhou-era states, located in modern day Hénán
Zhèngdé	明正德	Emperor of China who lived 1491-1521
Zhèng Méng	正蒙	Correcting Ignorance, an essay came from a work completed by Zhang in 1076
Zhēnrén	真人	Perfected person
Zhī	智	knowledge
zhīxíng héyī	知行合一	Wang Yangming's theory of "the unity of knowledge and action"
Zhōng Yōng	中庸	The Doctrine of the Mean (one of the Four Books)
Zhōngguó	中国	China, the Middle Kingdom
Zhōngguó Zhéxué Shǐ	中国哲学史	A Short History of Chinese Philosophy by Feng Youlan
Zhōu	周	The dynasty that followed the Shang...ran a long time, from 1046 BCE to 256 BCE

Zhōu Dūnyí	周敦颐	One of the five founders of Neo Confucianism during the Northern Song, lived 1017 to 1073
Zhōu Gōng	周公	The Duke of Zhou, son of King Wen and brother to Zhou King Wu
Zhou King Líng	周灵王	Reigned 571-545 BCE, when Confucius was born.
Zhòu Xīn	商纣辛	The equally venal final king of the Shang Dynasty, 1075-1046 BCE
Zhōu Yì	周易	The Changes of Zhou
Zhōulǐ	周礼	Rites of Zhou
Zhū Xī	朱熹	One of the all-time greats of Confucianism, lived 1130-1200
Zhū Yuánzhāng	朱元璋	Also known as Ming Taizu, the founder of the Ming Dynasty
Zhuāng Zhōu	庄周	Zhuangzi's name
Zhuāngzǐ	庄子	Daoist philosopher as well as the book that bears his name, also known as the Second Book of the Tao. He lived 369-286 BCE
Zhūzǐ	朱子	Master Zhū, an honorific name for Zhu Xi
Zhūzǐ Bǎijiā	诸子百家	The One Hundred Schools of Thought
Zǐ	子	Classical Chinese term for Master
Zǐ Gòng	子贡	Another major disciple of Confucius
Zǐ Sī	子思	Lived 481-402 BCE - Grandson of Confucius, teacher to Mengzi and Confucianism's most famous disciple
Zōu	邹国	Tiny state in SW Shandong that bordered Lǔ to the south
Zōu Yǎn	邹衍	Zhou era figure. Needham called him the Father of Chinese Scientific Thought. Lived from 305 to 240 BCE

Zūnchēng	尊称	an honorific or respectful term added to your surname.
Zuǒ Qiūmíng	左丘明	Writer of the Commentaries on the Chūn Qiū, a.k.a. the Zuǒ Zhuàn (左传)
Zuǒ Zhuàn	左传	The Commentary of Zuo (by Zuo Qiuming, 30 chapter work covering the period from 722-468 BCE

www.ingramcontent.com/pod-product-compliance
Lightning Source LLC
LaVergne TN
LVHW012022060526
838201LV00061B/4412